Cycling the
**Pennine
Bridleway**

ABOUT THE AUTHOR

Originally hailing from Sunderland, Keith's early interest was in white-water and sea canoeing. After a spell trekking in Nepal and canoe guiding in France, a teaching job in Kendal established him firmly in the Lake District. Walking, rock climbing and cycling became his new passions until a chance introduction to caving led to a rekindled love affair with the Yorkshire Dales. The last 20 years have been a delightful exploration of the lesser-known parts of these two areas, either underground with helmet and lamp, or above, on his (t)rusty mountain bike. Keith is a member of the Outdoor Writers and Photographers Guild and prides himself on an unrivalled knowledge of the bridleways of the Lake District and the Northern Dales.

Cycling the
Pennine
Bridleway

by Keith Bradbury

© Keith Bradbury 2012
First edition 2012
ISBN: 978 1 85284 655 8

Printed in China
on behalf of Latitude Press Ltd.

Published by Cicerone
2 Police Square, Milnthorpe
Cumbria LA7 7PY
www.cicerone.co.uk

A catalogue record for this book is
available from the British Library.
All photographs are by the author
unless otherwise stated.

This product includes mapping data
licensed from Ordnance Survey® with
the permission of the Controller of Her
Majesty's Stationery Office. © Crown
copyright 2012. All rights reserved.
Licence number PU100012932.

Dedication

Dedicated to the memory of my father,
JE Bradbury, who first nurtured in me a
love of the Dales.

Front cover: The final descent to
Ravenstonedale from the summit of
High Dolphinsty (Yorkshire Dales Part 3)
Title page: The bridleway leaving Tommy
Road (Section 3 Route 11; photo: EA
Bowness)
Back cover: Dropping off Giggleswick
Scar towards Feizor (Section 3 Route 2)

Advice to readers

While every effort is made by our authors
to ensure the accuracy of guidebooks
as they go to print, changes can occur
during the lifetime of an edition. If we
know of any, there will be an Updates
tab on this book's page on the Cicerone
website (www.cicerone.co.uk), so please
check before planning your trip. We
also advise that you check information
about such things as transport,
accommodation and shops locally. Even
rights of way can be altered over time.
We are always grateful for information
about any discrepancies between a
guidebook and the facts on the ground,
sent by email to info@cicerone.co.uk
or by post to Cicerone, 2 Police Square,
Milnthorpe LA7 7PY, United Kingdom.

Acknowledgements

Many thanks to Julie Thompson from
the Pennine Bridleway team and Mark
Allum from Yorkshire Dales National
Park for their untiring support and
supplying information about continuing
developments. To Sue Viccars, Neil
Simpson, Lois Sparling and the Cicerone
team who guided me so painlessly
through the publishing process. To Ted
Bowness, Geoff Cater, Steve Bramall
and Nick Crosby for their stunning
photography, which so ably captures
the nature of the ride. And finally, to that
group of reprobates I shudder to call
friends, who supported me so warmly by
chortling at my route descriptions and
laughing hysterically whenever I fell off!

Contents

A leafy lane in spring, outside Feizor (Section 3 Route 2)

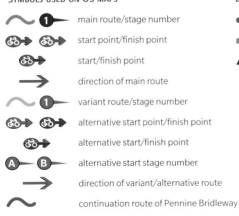

APPENDICES

SYMBOLS USED ON OS MAPS

~ **1** → main route/stage number

🚲→ 🚲→ start point/finish point

🚲→ start/finish point

→ direction of main route

~ **1** variant route/stage number

🚲→ 🚲→ alternative start point/finish point

🚲→ alternative start/finish point

A—**B**— alternative start stage number

→ direction of variant/alternative route

~ continuation route of Pennine Bridleway

→ direction of Pennine Bridleway

For full OS symbols key see OS maps.

DIFFICULTY GRADES

● easy

■ medium

▲ hard

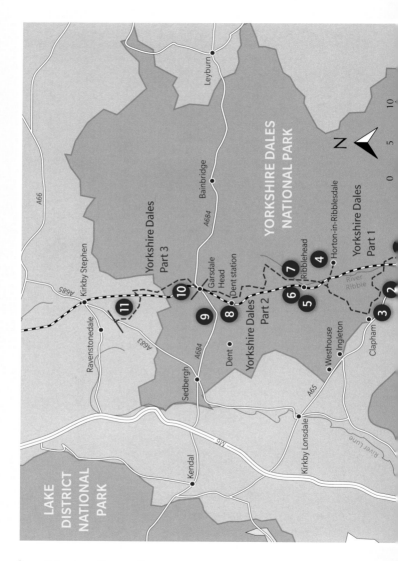

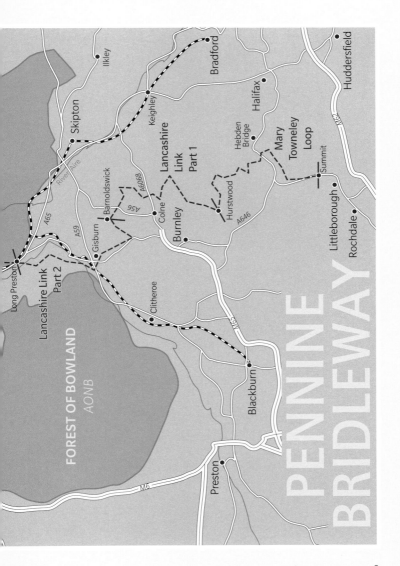

PENNINE BRIDLEWAY

FOREST OF BOWLAND
AONB

Lancashire Link Part 2

Lancashire
Link
Part 1

Mary
Towneley
Loop

Ilkley

Bradford

Huddersfield

Skipton

Keighley

Halifax

Hebden
Bridge

Summit

River Aire

Barnoldswick

Colne

Burnley

Hurstwood

Littleborough

Gisburn

Rochdale

Long Preston

A65

A59

A56

A6068

A646

Clitheroe

M65

Blackburn

Preston

M6

M62

This is Cumbrian Limestone, not Yorkshire (Section 3 Route 11)

Introduction

Imagine a 560km (350-mile) National Trail, running along the spine of England from Derbyshire to Northumberland and specifically designed to be accessible to a wide range of users. Gates that open easily; surfaces that are regularly maintained and repaired; signposts and route guides show the way.

The good news is that such a route has been under development for several years, and that the next section is now open for riding! The 188km (117-mile) southern section of the Pennine Bridleway National Trail, running from Derbyshire to the south Pennines, is now well established and has been enthusiastically received. Work on the next major section of bridleway, through the stunning scenery of the Yorkshire Dales, has been in progress since 2002 and is now complete: almost 145km (90 miles) of quality trail (plus the bonus of the 74km/46-mile Mary Towneley Loop) for those who may be seeking even more adventure.

This guide provides a description of this latest extension to the Pennine Bridleway: firstly around part of the already established Mary Towneley Loop in Calderdale and then on, through the beautiful Yorkshire Dales, to the current terminus on the outskirts of Ravenstonedale, near Kirkby Stephen in Cumbria.

Just follow those signs – but which way?

The guide is divided into three sections:

Section 1 The Mary Towneley Loop (MTL) is described in an anti-clockwise direction, from Summit (near Littleborough) where the Derbyshire section of the Pennine Bridleway reaches the southernmost point of the loop. This rotation gives the shortest distance when heading northwards to locate the continuation of the Pennine Bridleway towards the Yorkshire Dales.

Section 2 A linear description of the new section of the Pennine Bridleway, beginning at the northernmost tip of the MTL (Hurstwood Reservoir, near Burnley). The guide breaks the route down into five sections, each a suggested 'day-length' ride, but also giving details for those riders wishing to travel the whole route in a continuous journey.

- The Lancashire Link Part 1, from the top of the MTL to Barnoldswick
- The Lancashire Link Part 2 – Barnoldswick to Long Preston
- The Yorkshire Dales Part 1 – Long Preston to Horton-in-Ribblesdale
- The Yorkshire Dales Part 2 – Horton-in-Ribblesdale to Garsdale Head
- The Yorkshire Dales Part 3 – Garsdale Head to Ravenstonedale

Section 3 This section is for those riders who do not wish to ride the whole route as a linear trail. It splits the main bridleway into 11 'day routes', 12–25.75km (8–16 miles) in length. However, each individual day route links at some point with the next, so that by riding all 11 routes the whole of the Yorkshire section of the Pennine Bridleway will be covered.

Crossing the Ribble on Cow Bridge (The Lancashire Link Part 1; photo: Geoff Cater)

WHERE TO START?

The simple answer to this question is – how long have you got? The full Pennine Bridleway starts at Middleton Top, near Matlock in Derbyshire but this guide is primarily concerned with the section passing through the Yorkshire Dales (from Long Preston to Ravenstonedale). For completeness the shortest circuit around the Mary Towneley Loop

and the new link between the top of the MTL (at Hurstwood) and Long Preston has been included. These northern Lancashire sections have their own charm and are worthwhile rides in their own right, but for many do not match the pastoral beauty and spectacular limestone scenery of the Yorkshire Dales.

The northernmost point of the Mary Towneley Loop is often seen as a natural starting point because it marks the end of current route development and the beginning of the new extension. Starting the ride from Hurstwood Reservoir, on the outskirts of Burnley, gives an excellent introduction to the overall route: wild, rugged, gritstone scenery across Extwistle Moor and over to Barnoldswick, before more gentle terrain across the pastoral farmland of Gisburn and Paythorn, marking the run into Long Preston.

From Long Preston however, the mighty uplift of the Craven Fault dictates that steep climbs are the order of the day as the limestone scars and craggy peaks make their presence felt. With the climbs however, come the views; and the true nature of Dales scenery opens out ahead as the climb from Long Preston surmounts the rise alongside the abandoned quarries at Hunter Bark. This is Yorkshire at its best: enjoy your ride!

The northern extension

Ravestonedale is the current end of the Pennine Bridleway, but the full route has always been intended to reach Byrness in Northumberland, just a few miles from the mighty Kielder Reservoir. However, other than official approval of a preferred route, work has not yet started on this northern extension and considering the current financial climate it is no longer envisaged that even preliminary work on the project will begin within the foreseeable future. 'Watch this space' is the key phrase here: should financial aid become available, full details will be posted on the Pennine Bridleway website.

GETTING THERE

Picking up the existing route at Summit

The Derbyshire section of the Pennine Bridleway links with the Mary Towneley Loop at the village of Summit, near Littleborough, Rochdale. To find this point by car, follow the M62 (trans-Pennine motorway) to Junction 20 (Rochdale and Oldham). The only exit from Junction 20 is onto another motorway, the A627(M), which should be followed northwards towards Rochdale. After 1.6km the motorway ends at a roundabout with the A664; follow this to the left for a short distance to a junction with the A58. Turn right along the A58 for 7.2km into Littleborough. Just past Littleborough railway station the A58 turns right where the A6033 bears off left. Take the A6033 and continue for a further 2.4km into Summit, where the Pennine Bridleway will be found crossing the A6033, alongside the Rochdale Canal, immediately beyond The Summit Inn.

If wanting to access the route by rail, a half-hourly service runs Monday–Saturday from Littleborough (Northern Rail: tel: 08450 000125) to Manchester Victoria to the west and Leeds to the east. Hourly services operate on evenings and Sundays. There are plans to improve the service towards Manchester by the reinstatement of the former south-to-west curve at Todmorden, providing a rail link westwards to Burnley.

Hurstwood Reservoir and The Mary Towneley Loop

Hurstwood Reservoir (near where Section 1, The Mary Towneley Loop, links with Section 2, The Lancashire Link) is located a few miles from the centre of Burnley, just north of the A646 Burnley-to-Todmorden road. Burnley is well served by road and rail services, which makes getting to the area relatively easy. If travelling southwards on the M6, leave at Junction 30 onto the M61, if heading northwards, access onto the M61 will be from Junction 29.

Just one slip and...! (Section 3 Route 3; photo: Geoff Cater)

Almost immediately, leave the M61 at Junction 2 onto the M65 towards Blackburn, Accrington and Burnley. Follow the M65 for a further 25.5km to Junction 9, where an exit can be made onto the A646 towards Todmorden. A left turn in the village of Walk Mill leads onto country lanes, where Hurstwood will be found a few miles to the north.

Burnley (approximately 6.4km from Hurstwood) also has a railway station, which can be accessed via Preston on the West Coast main line.

Colne Station is the terminus of the East Lancashire line, which also serves Burnley: Colne lies 5.6km west of Wycoller Country Park (Lancashire Link Part 1). North of this point, however, there is no railway access to the Pennine Bridleway until the Settle–Carlisle line is met at Long Preston.

Long Preston

By car, Long Preston (accessing Section 2, The Yorkshire Dales) can be reached via the A65. This busy trunk road runs from Junction 36 of the M6 (near Kendal) through to Skipton to the east, and then on towards the major conurbations of Leeds and Bradford.

By rail, Long Preston can be accessed via the famously picturesque Settle–Carlisle line, while another small branch line runs from Lancaster to join the Settle–Carlisle line at Long Preston.

Please note however, that while all the railways in this region allow cycles to be carried, many have restrictions on the number of bikes carried on any single train. The decision as to how many cyclists will be allowed on a given service often depends upon how busy the train is and how accommodating the guard happens to be. Cycles can be booked in advance and this is definitely recommended, but larger groups wishing to travel on the same train may face difficulties because of these limitations. Always check with the relevant railway company before planning your trip.

Who is this guide for?

Whereas the Pennine Bridleway has been set up as a multi-purpose route (for cyclists, horse riders and walkers) this guide – although of interest to the latter two groups of user – has been written specifically for mountain bikers. Cyclists using this guide should be aware at all times that they are likely to come across other users at times, and behave accordingly by alerting both walkers and horse riders (carefully) to their presence, and not hurtling past at top speed (see 'Rules of the road' at the end of this section).

Long-distance trail enthusiasts

The opening of this section of the Pennine Bridleway presents a fantastic new opportunity for those keen to tackle the next stage of this long-distance route.

Day riders

Linear routes can be difficult for mountain bikers. The logistics of arranging transport at each end of the ride are often problematic, particularly if the trail crosses into a different valley, when the return journey by road can be laborious. This is not a problem on the Yorkshire section of the Pennine Bridleway, because the trail follows the route of the Settle–Carlisle railway. Each day-long section begins and ends close to a station, while many also pass other stations en route: perfect for dealing with mishaps or breakdowns.

In addition, many of the routes in this guide are currently unknown even to local riders because they are reliant on new bridleways; some upgraded from existing footpaths, others that are sections of completely new trail across virgin countryside.

The circular routes have been limited to 12–25.75km in length to encourage novice cyclists to get out there and have a go. Newcomers and family groups should find each ride well within their capabilities but, because each individual route connects to the next, two or even three loops can be linked together to provide rides of increasing levels of difficulty for those who seek a greater challenge.

These trails have a huge advantage in that most have been recently developed and improved to be well-drained, well-surfaced and quagmire-free! Even in typical British weather conditions there should be no major problems as far as riding surfaces are concerned. However, it must be remembered that the northern Pennines enjoy their fair share of hazardous weather conditions: underestimate this potential danger at your peril. In this respect, late

Spring arrives at last!

spring, summer and early autumn are the ideal times to plan an expedition in order to see the Dales at their best – balmy days bathed in sunshine, with the haunting call of the curlew echoing overhead. However, these same routes ridden in the depths of winter can be magical experiences: Ingleborough wreathed in snow, with your tyre tracks the only sign that anyone has been this way before.

Prevailing winds tend to come from the west and this may influence the choice of route on a blustery day. Also, once off the main bridleway, the trails are not as well maintained and limestone surfaces can be treacherously slippery after rain. Areas that may be particularly boggy in wet conditions are noted in the route descriptions, not only because it can be very hard work riding across sinking moss but also because these surfaces are particularly subject to erosion and need to be avoided when they are most at risk after prolonged rainfall.

In terms of how busy the Pennine Bridleway might be at any particular time, the Mary Towneley Loop has been established for a number of years and has become more popular as guidebooks and magazine articles have been published. However, even on weekends and school holidays, you are only likely to meet a few walkers and a couple of mountain bike groups on a day's ride. The new sections of trail north of Hurstwood are largely unknown except to local riders who have seen the new developments taking place and have investigated whether the trails were available to ride. Here you can often ride all day and not meet another user.

This situation will clearly change as word of this new trail spreads, and this guide is an inevitable part of that process! Occasionally, competitions and events are held on popular sections such as the MTL or the Three Peaks, flooding the area with competitors and spectators; accommodation and parking will be in very great demand. A quick phone call to local Tourist Information offices will soon establish whether any events are planned, and you would be well advised to do so before firming up your final travel dates.

ACCOMMODATION

There are a number of key towns and villages on the main route. Settle (near Long Preston at the start of the Yorkshire Dales section) and Kirkby Stephen (a few miles away from the end of the ride at Ravenstonedale) are the only centres offering extensive amenities. Elsewhere, the larger villages such as Austwick, Clapham, Horton and Ravenstonedale offer accommodation, pubs and village shops. Other centres like Dent and Hawes are feasible stop-off points but to reach them will require significant diversions from the main route.

The Mary Towneley Loop and the route onwards to Barnoldswick tend to be nearer towns and villages where short diversions can be made to find supplies or accommodation. The Long Preston to Horton-in-Ribblesdale section is also well serviced and should offer no problems for lunch or somewhere to rest that weary head. Most places are happy to offer single-night accommodation during weekdays, but some will have a two-night minimum stay policy at weekends (these restrictions may be negotiable outside the main tourist season from late August through to spring).

North of Horton is likely to present more difficulties. A short diversion can be made to bunkhouse accommodation at Gearstones or Ribblehead, where the Station Inn offers good food and an attached bunkhouse. Garsdale Head, at the end of this section, has no shops and limited accommodation. The Moorcock Inn is excellent for food and cycle-friendly accommodation, as is the attached bed-and-breakfast establishment, but once those beds have been booked there are very few alternative facilities within the area. This shortage may well change as the Pennine Bridleway becomes more popular and extra facilities are established, but at the moment advance booking, well ahead of your trip, is essential. Remember too that pressures on these limited facilities will be even greater during weekends (particularly Bank Holidays) and school holidays.

From Garsdale Head to Ravenstonedale the trail is remote with no facilities. The Moorcock Inn will make up an excellent packed lunch for your journey but you will need to be self-sufficient until Ravenstonedale is reached. Here a village shop and three excellent pubs offer all the necessary facilities.

The Pennine Bridleway team offer a comprehensive list of possibilities on their website (www.nationaltrail.co.uk/penninebridleway) and this excellent resource is updated regularly. Local Tourist Information Centres also keep extensive lists of accommodation possibilities for all needs and are usually extremely helpful (see also Appendix D Accommodation).

Will he make it? – or won't he?
(photo: Steve Bramall)

SAFETY

Be under no illusion. A great deal of the Pennine Bridleway has been designed to avoid roads and villages. Mobile phones will frequently have no signal and the nearest road or settlement may well be a few miles of arduous riding away. In these situations, it is essential that each group should plan carefully for unexpected situations.

If an unexpected breakdown requires a push of a few kilometres to the nearest village it would be inconvenient, but not particularly disastrous. However, even a small tumble on slippery limestone could result in a broken wrist or dislocated shoulder, and a much more serious situation. How will you summon help if your mobile phone has no signal? Who will stay with the casualty? Are

Sometimes it's just easier to push!
(photo: Steve Bramall)

you carrying a basic first aid kit? Does anyone know how to use it? Do you have an emergency shelter? How will you prevent hypothermia setting in with an immobile patient on a cold, wet, windy day?

Remember that an ambulance will be no use if you are halfway up Whernside on a single-track bridleway. In case of emergency in remote locations, call 999 and ask for Cave and Fell Rescue. They will have the expertise, equipment and vehicles to reach you where a normal ambulance would fear to tread. Remember also that a rescue team will need to know where you are. A location of 'somewhere just outside Garsdale' will not be much help to the fell rescue team, so make sure that all members of your group can read a map and work out a basic map reference (see also Appendix C Useful contacts).

HOW FAR CAN I RIDE IN A DAY?

Off-road cycling is considerably more strenuous than riding a road bike with narrow tyres on a pristine tarmac surface. The suggested day sections in this guide should be manageable for a cyclist of average fitness who has a limited experience of off-road cycling. However, if you were still at school the last time you rode a bike and that was only to zoom down to the shops on your Raleigh Grifter, you may struggle with the distances and climbs encountered on the ride.

The answer, of course, is to get out and ride! Try some local routes,

Ribblehead Viaduct from Bruntscar (Section 3 Route 6)

Should you feel that the suggested distances are going to be too much for some members of your group, there are plenty of opportunities to shorten the suggested day lengths. For example, the first day of the Lancashire Link, from Hurstwood to Long Preston, could easily be split by planning an overnight stop around Barnoldswick. The correspondingly more gentle second day, from Barnoldswick to Long Preston, could then be extended as far as Settle or Stainforth, thus consequently making an easier day over to Horton-in Ribblesdale. From Horton, the trail becomes more remote. However, a short diversion from the junction on Cam High Road, gives an easy downhill sprint to the bunkhouse at High Gearstones, or a little further along the road to the Station Inn (and attached bunkhouse) at Ribblehead. The final day, from Garsdale Head to Ravenstonedale, appears at first sight to be an easy one; but be cautious here. Although the first section up to Lady Anne's Highway is a manageable climb, the second big ascent of the day, up to the High Dolphinsty pass, is anything but gentle and can feel disproportionately strenuous if it comes at the end of a number of days of hard riding!

preferably those that give an indication of distance and height gain. These experiences will quickly show you how tough a ride of 14 or 15km and 300m of climbing will feel on your legs, lungs and backside! Once you have an idea of your fitness a few more rides will soon confirm your personal limits and you will know which of the rides in this guide to tackle.

A little 'pre-training' will quickly have unexpected benefits: you will be surprised at how rapidly fitness level improves, and routes that seem taxing at first soon become much easier. Like all physical activity, practice makes perfect, and you will enjoy the Pennine Bridleway much more if you feel confident and physically prepared for it.

WHAT TYPE OF BIKE WILL I NEED?

There is no need to go out and buy a £7000 carbon-fibre dream-machine, but there are points to consider when assessing whether your existing mountain bike is suitable for the route. Although the trails are generally well maintained, there are some sections that are muddy, rocky and testing. Front suspension is definitely recommended (but not essential) for personal comfort and quality of ride. Full suspension is ideal, but a cheap, full-suspension bike will almost certainly be less reliable than a similarly priced bike sporting only front suspension. If you are undecided do a tour of your local bike shops, explaining what your plans are, and ask for help. Most will give knowledgeable, largely impartial advice to prospective buyers because they will wish to keep you as a regular customer.

WAYMARKS AND ACCESS

Because the Pennine Bridleway is a National Trail, the symbol used throughout the route is an acorn (this includes the Mary Towneley Loop). The acorn symbol is frequently used in conjunction with coloured arrows to identify the legal status of that particular path. A yellow arrow indicates that only walkers are allowed to use the path; a blue arrow denotes that the trail is a bridleway and can therefore be used by walkers, cyclists and horses. Occasionally the acorn symbol may be seen alongside a red arrow, indicating that the track is a byway. In addition to walkers, cyclists and equestrian users, a byway is available for use by motorised traffic so be aware that off-road vehicles and trail bikes may appear on these sections of the route.

Remember that a number of sections of the Pennine Bridleway have only very recently been upgraded from existing footpaths or, more unusually, created across countryside where no right-of-way previously existed. Don't be too concerned if you glance at your trusty old map to find that you are

Pennine Bridleway signpost with Lambert Lane going off behind (photo: Geoff Cater)

cycling happily along a footpath and you have always understood that this was not allowed. Rest assured that, provided you are following the trails described in this guide, you will have full legal permission to ride.

USING THIS GUIDE

The Grading System

Each route description starts with a box of information relating to that day's ride, giving details of start and finish points, distance, amount of on- and off-road riding (and the off-road percentage for the day), ascent, suggested timing, relevant map(s), overall grading, access (nearest railway station) and pubs and/or cafés encountered en route.

The 'Overall grading' is denoted by ●, ■ or ▲.

- ● indicates that the climbs are fully rideable by a cyclist with a modest level of fitness and the corresponding descents will also be gentle enough to be tackled by a rider with relatively little cycling experience. ● would also indicate that the route offers generally smooth, graded tracks in good condition, giving little difficulty to riders of modest ability. Please remember however, that a prolonged spell of bad weather or a situation when farm vehicles have been using the trail could temporarily turn an easy track into quite a different proposition.

- ■ indicates a trail that would be a little more technical but that should still be within most people's capability. The steeper sections of climbing may require the odd push (until fitness levels improve), while the descents should be rideable (with care) once appropriate levels of confidence have developed.

- In comparison, a ▲ route would have most, if not all, riders pushing up some of the steepest parts of the climbs, and some sections of descent would only be manageable by experienced riders with high skill levels.

By way of example, in Route 2 (Feizor, Wharfe and Catrigg Force) the main route, returning via Feizor, gives largely gentle climbing with no technical difficulties. The riding surfaces are good, on easily followed trails, hence the 'easy' ● grading. The alternative return via Catrigg Force however, has an extra 300m of climbing, which is clearly going to be more strenuous (hence ■). In reality, this extra difficulty consists of a steep climb alongside Stainforth Beck. One or two sections of the climb have an occasional rocky step, which could demand a quick push – also reflected in the use of a ■ symbol.

Any type of grading system will inevitably be subjective. It must be remembered, however, that the aim of such a system is merely to give a datum point by which other routes can be judged; once you have tackled a couple of rides you should have a realistic awareness

Easy riding alongside Moughton Scars (Section 3 Route 3)

of how much harder a ■ or ▲ route is likely to be over the easier ● routes already ticked off.

Timings

Each route description has suggested timings for how long it should take to get around. These are necessarily a broad guide and the actual time to complete the route will depend upon fitness, experience, time of year and weather conditions. In addition, breakdowns, punctures and rest stops will all add significantly to the figure given. Please also remember that a five-hour ride, on fresh legs, after a good night's sleep, will feel very different to the same ride attempted at the end of a four-day expedition when backsides are tender and legs weary from prolonged effort.

Maps

Ordnance Survey (www.ordnance survey.co.uk/leisure) provides maps of the area covered in both 1:50,000 (Landranger) and 1:25,000 (Explorer) scales. Extracts from the most up-to-date 1:50,000 maps have been used in this guidebook, while each route information box lists the more detailed Explorer map (or maps) required for that ride. From south to north these are:

- OS Explorer OL21 South Pennines
- OS Explorer OL41 Forest of Bowland & Ribblesdale
- OS Explorer OL2 Yorkshire Dales (Southern & Western area)
- OS Explorer OL19 Howgill Fells & Upper Eden Valley

Equivalent Landranger maps covering the route are as follows:

- OS Landranger 103 Blackburn and Burnley (Mary Towneley Loop and Lancashire Link Parts 1 and 2)
- OS Landranger 98 Wensleydale and Upper Wharfedale (Yorkshire Dales Parts 1, 2 and 3)
- OS Landranger 91 Appleby-in-Westmorland (Yorkshire Dales Part 3)

Abbreviations and place names

In the route directions, 'left' and 'right' have been abbreviated to L or R, and 'straight ahead' to SA. North, South, East and West (when referring to compass points) appear as N, S, E and W. In similar fashion, the Pennine Bridleway is shortened to PB and the Mary Towneley Loop to MTL. Some place names are shown in bold text,

The traverse around Birkett Common, alongside the River Eden (Section 3 Route 11)

for example **Settle**. This indicates that the particular place name is featured on the relevant 1:50,000 Ordnance Survey Landranger map. Place names not shown in bold do not appear on the 1:50,000 maps but may be shown on the larger scaled 1:25,000 Explorer maps. The route descriptions show roads as **A646**. Important signs along the way are noted in *red italics*, with easy to miss paths to look out for in **bold green** and warnings in **bold red**.

WHAT TO TAKE

Before starting the ride it is important to make sure that not only are you prepared physically, but also that you know what items are essential to take with you. Inevitably, a long-distance ride is going to be a compromise between what items you may need and what you are prepared to carry. Some groups use a support vehicle (or even tow a trailer) to carry bags, spares, provisions and so on, while others choose to be self-sufficient and load their bikes down with panniers and rucksacks.

It is also possible to leave a support car at each night-stop by doing a bit of to-ing and fro-ing with cars the day before each ride. Although somewhat time consuming it does mean that injuries or breakdowns are easy to deal with and transport is on hand at the end of the ride.

Basic checklist – essential kit

- Bike
- Helmet
- Cycling clothes
- Gloves
- Footwear
- Waterproofs
- Goggles
- Rucksack
- First aid kit
- Mini toolkit
- Chain splitter/quick link
- Replacement drop out (on which hangs the derailleur, designed to bend or snap in a collision)
- Spare tube/s
- Puncture repair kit
- Decent bike pump
- Duct tape
- Guidebook
- Map/s
- Snacks/food
- Drinks/hydration bladder
- Wallet (money and cards)
- Mobile phone
- Camera

The following items could make the difference between an enjoyable day's ride and a nightmare push back to civilisation. People with similar makes of bike can share kit: one takes a spare chain, another spare brake pads, and so on. The following items have proved to be lifesavers (see also Appendix E Bike shops).

- Couple of extra inner tubes and puncture repair kit
- New chain
- Brake pads
- Gear cable and brake cable
- Oil/grease/spray lubricant
- Spare derailleur between two or three bikes
- Selection of more specialised bike tools for overnight emergency repairs (such as a big hammer and wrench)

A spare tyre could be left in your 'pub bag' so you could change a damaged tyre at the overnight stop.

If using a support vehicle the following items could be taken for overnight stops.

- Change of clothing for the evening
- Dry/clean cycling kit
- Washing kit/personal hygiene
- Towel
- Extra spare parts

Not everyone makes it across the ford! (Section 3 Route 3; photo: Geoff Cater)

Rules of the road

These simple rules have been developed by the International Mountain Biking Association (IMBA) and are designed to minimise conflict with other trail users, land-owners and legal bodies. Like all codes of behaviour they are largely common sense and are followed as a matter of course by all but the most confrontational of cyclists. Please help to keep our trails open by setting a good example of environmentally sound and socially responsible off-road cycling.

Only ride on legal trails

This generally means bridleways, byways open to all traffic (BOATs) green lanes, some forest tracks and paths, but absolutely **not** footpaths. Respect trail and road closures (ask for information if uncertain); avoid trespassing on private land; obtain permits or other authorisation as may be required. Remember that the way we ride may well influence future trail management decisions and policies.

Leave no trace

Be sensitive to the terrain beneath your wheels. Recognise different types of soils and trail construction; practise low-impact cycling. Wet and muddy trails are more vulnerable to damage. When the trail is soft, consider other riding options. This also means staying on existing trails and not creating new ones. Don't cut across hairpins. In short: take nothing but photographs and leave nothing but tyre tracks.

Control your bike!

Inattention for even a second can cause problems. Stick to any bike speed recommendations and always ride within your own capabilities.

Give way to other users

Let your fellow trail users know you're coming. A friendly greeting or bell is considerate and works well; don't startle others. Show your respect when passing, by slowing to a walking pace or even stopping. Anticipate other trail users around corners or in blind spots. Slow down, establish communication, be prepared to stop if necessary and pass safely.

Never scare animals

All animals are startled by an unannounced approach, a sudden movement, or a loud noise. This can be dangerous for you, others on the trail and the animals. Give animals extra space and time to adjust to you. When passing horses use special care and follow directions from their riders – ask if uncertain. 'Chasing' farmstock and disturbing wildlife can be a serious offence. Leave gates as you found them, or as marked.

Plan ahead

Know your equipment, your ability and the area in which you are riding – and prepare accordingly. Be self-sufficient at all times, keep equipment in good repair and carry necessary supplies for changes in weather or other conditions. A well-executed trip should be a satisfying experience for you (and not a burden to others). Always wear a helmet and appropriate safety gear.

Steady climbing on a stone-set trail, with Rochdale in the background

A picture of concentration

The Mary Towneley Loop
Summit to Hurstwood (anti-clockwise)

START	Junction with the MTL at Summit, NE of Rochdale SD 944 189
FINISH	Hurstwood Reservoir car park SD 882 312
DISTANCE	29km (18 miles)
OFF ROAD	25km (15½ miles)
ON ROAD	4km (2½ miles)
ASCENT	1005m (3300ft)
TIME	6–8hrs
MAP	OS Explorer OL21 South Pennines
OVERALL GRADING	■
ACCESS	See Introduction
PUBS	The Summit Inn, Summit; the Top Brink Inn, Lumbutts
CAFÉS	None en route

85% OFF ROAD

The Derbyshire section of the Pennine Bridleway links with the Mary Towneley Loop at Summit, near Littleborough on the outskirts of Rochdale. Adding this circular loop to the linear trail from Derbyshire gives the route a shape similar to a tennis racquet, with the MTL forming the 'head'. If planning to follow the Pennine Bridleway on towards Yorkshire, however, a choice has to be made at Summit: whether to turn left (clockwise) or right (anti-clockwise), since the onward route leaves the Mary Towneley Loop at Hurstwood on its northern edge.

Aficionados of the MTL will have their own favourite rotation and will no doubt be able to justify their reasoning to those who prefer to go around the other way. The rationale followed in this guidebook is simple: the anti-clockwise route described is the shortest way to reach Hurstwood. The MTL is a challenging route in its own right and, although less than half is completed, it is both steep and rugged in places.

map continues on p34

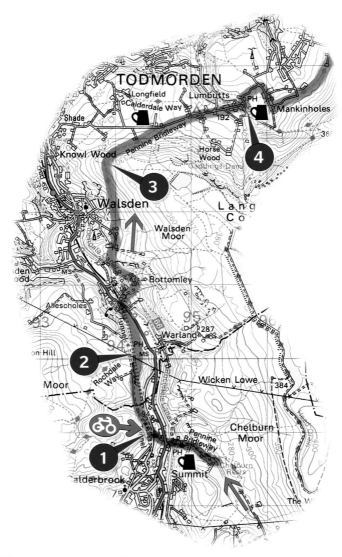

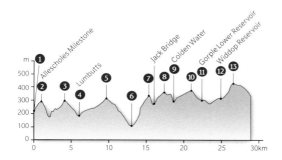

The final part of the Derbyshire section of the PB, heading north towards the MTL, runs alongside Lower Chelburn Reservoir to arrive at Summit Lock, the highest point on the **Rochdale Canal**. Cross the bridge over the canal by The Summit Inn and continue uphill to reach the `A6033`. Use the Pegasus crossing to gain the other side of the road, then turn **R** along the wide pavement for about 20m. At a house on the left (Windy Ridge) turn **L** up a very narrow path, and climb steeply to a grassy area by another house.

Keeping the house on the right and the stables on the left, continue up to the drive, with a high gritstone wall left, to meet the start of the MTL at a tarmac lane (the Calderbrook Road, mainly for access to farms and houses). In a prominent position at the junction sits a large, round tower, a ventilation shaft for the railway running through Summit Tunnel below.

DIRECTIONS

1. Having now joined the MTL, turn **R** up the Calderbrook Road but, almost immediately, leave it again by bearing off **L** onto a rough gravel track, heading uphill. At a cattle grid take the **R** fork. Continue to climb steadily on the gravel path, taking care not to cross the wire fence to the right, protecting a **potentially dangerous section of cliff edge**. Just beyond this section a gate is reached with fine views back to the Chelburn Reservoirs. Continue climbing, albeit more gently now, with a fence left and wall right.

The Allescholes Milestone on Reddyshore Scout

Pass through a metal gate and cross a bridge, directly under a line of electricity pylons: look carefully to the right to find the ancient **Allescholes Milestone**, which marks an important change in direction.

2 Pass to the right of the milestone, then zigzag steeply downhill. Pass through a couple of gates, leading eventually to a junction. Turn **R** onto the farm road and, at the next junction of paths, drop downhill along the fenced track to meet the busy `A6033`. Cross the road at the Pegasus crossing, then turn **L** along the verge. The first turning on the **R** will be a tarmac lane (Bottomley Road), which runs downhill, away from the `A6033`. Follow the lane between cottages, then **R** over the canal bridge at Bottomley Lock.

Keep **SA** between houses onto a narrow, stone-paved packhorse route that climbs steeply up towards the hamlet of **Bottomley**. The stone-setted, walled path narrows and steepens considerably as it runs between fields. Pass through a five-bar field gate onto a tarmac lane alongside Sweetbriar Cottage on the right.

Pass the cottage uphill to enter the hamlet, but almost immediately take another (signposted) **L** turn, between the houses to enter another causeway – known locally as a 'causey' – which drops quickly to cross a stream on a railed bridge.

A grassy embankment now runs towards Dean Royd Farm, keeping to the right of the farm buildings. The narrow causey then steepens to run uphill, following a wall on the left to reach a wooden gate. Follow the continuing trail of stone flags to meet a farm track at a field gate.

Bear **L** onto the track and pass through another gate, alongside a white property on the right. Turn **L** again, keeping the white house on the right, and follow the tarmac lane to a bend at North Hollingworth Farm. On this bend fork **R**, heading uphill towards the entrances to some houses (the last house on the right has a red telephone box in the garden).

3 On approaching the drive of this last house look for a waymarked trail going off **L** alongside the gardens. Follow this as it drops a little, then begin a steep and lengthy ascent along the elevated stone causeway of Salter Rake Gate, eventually contouring around Rake End. Eventually, however, a bumpy descent – still on the familiar stone causeway – meets tarmac at a farm gate approaching Hey Head Farm.

Note The Shepherd's Rest pub can be found a few yards to the left here.

To continue the route turn **R** along the tarmac lane, with Hey Head Farm left. Follow the road downhill for 2.5km into **Lumbutts** village to a point where, just beyond the bridge, the road takes a sharp right turn.

4 On the **L** here (**partially obscured by trees and bushes**) there is an extremely steep and narrow packhorse route, which climbs up the causey to The Top Brink public house. Go straight across the road here onto a continuation of the narrow, paved bridleway, which ascends to meet the road directly opposite the cemetery and an old Methodist Sunday school, now converted to a dwelling house.

Peaceful perambulation in Callis Wood

Turn **R** along the road to enter the hamlet of **Mankinholes**, passing the Youth Hostel (left). At the far end of the hamlet, on a bend just beyond a series of water troughs, a bridleway goes off straight ahead, but turn sharp **L** here on the MTL.

Running between stone walls, the trail climbs up the hill towards **Stoodley Pike** where, after a long, steady ascent, it thankfully swings rightwards to follow the contours of the hill below the monument, on an old packhorse trail (London Road). After a sharp **LH** turn the gradient eases and the trail continues towards Swillington Farm, crossing the Pennine Way just before the farm is reached.

5 At Swillington Farm a gate leads to a continuation of the bridleway down a wide, walled, farm lane to a staggered junction of tracks.

Note The next section of track is a new alternative to earlier versions of the PB, which once continued via Erringden Grange and Horsehold. Both new and old routes soon reunite at the packhorse bridge in Callis Wood.

From the staggered junction a gravel farm track goes off to the **L**, passing the buildings of Kershaw Farm where it then turns sharp **R** onto the grassy surface of Pinnacle Lane. Easy riding continues for about 800m to where a farm gate bars further progress and the continuation of the lane straight ahead (a footpath) looks uninvitingly overgrown. At this point the PB turns **L** through a gate alongside a stream, onto a new track, running downhill. The new bridleway gives easy riding alongside the stream until the track bears **R** and enters the first trees of Callis Wood.

The track now becomes a little muddier and turns sharp **L** to a gate and packhorse bridge over the stream (the path coming straight towards the gate is the original route of the PB dropping down from the hamlet of Horsehold).

Climbing steeply out of the valley beyond the bridge, a footpath is met coming in from the left (Pennine Way). Both paths now join and are followed to the **R**, beginning a zigzag descent to the valley floor through Callis Wood.

After a short distance bear **R** off the farm road, taking a softer track through the trees, before rejoining the track some 400m further down the hill. Continue to follow the good track downwards, swinging around a sharp **RH** bend in front of a house, then around an equally sharp **LH** bend to a gate next to a cattle grid. Beyond the cattle grid the track continues easily down the hill to meet a canal bridge at **Charlestown**.

map continues on p38

But everyone is wearing them this year, darling!
(photo: Geoff Cater)

A pleasant lunch stop above Callis Wood

6 Use the bridge to cross the Rochdale Canal, then the River Calder.

Note The canal towpath to the right can be followed to Hebden Bridge if supplies are required (2.8km detour).

Cross the busy **A646** via a Pegasus crossing. Once over the road turn **L**, using the fenced section of trail running parallel to the road for 200m, where a **R** turn will be found leading onto Jumble Hole Road. This tarmac road quickly passes under the railway line then becomes a gravel lane between houses as it begins to climb steadily, with a stream on the left.

Still climbing, the track runs steeply through mixed woodland on a double concrete track. As the gradient finally begins to level off and the riding surface becomes tarmac, look carefully for a **L** turn onto a narrow packhorse trail, heading uphill into the trees (identified by an easily missed **blue PB marker post**).

Follow this narrow packhorse trail as it zigzags very steeply uphill to meet a gate at the entrance to Dove Scout Farm on the left. At the farm entrance bear **R**, following the main farm road as it leads steadily uphill to eventually meet a tarmac road (Badger Lane).

7 Turn **L** along the lane for 50m before taking the first bridleway on the **R** (alongside Bracewell Hall), which climbs again, between houses, to the top of the hill. Once on the summit descend a long, straight, narrow path, but **take care!** A stone bollard in the middle of the path marks the crossing point of the Calderdale Way footpath; hitting this at full tilt would certainly make for some spectacular aerobatics.

A crossroads is met at the bottom of the hill, in front of the house at Shaw Bottom. Bear **L** here, then immediately **R** again to pass beside the house. At the bottom of this next small slope meet Shaw Bottom Lane and turn **L** along it, with the stream of Colden Water running alongside on the right.

After 300m Shaw Bottom Lane meets a tarmac road (Shaw New Road) just before the New Delight Inn at **Jack Bridge**. Turn **L** here and start the climb up the road towards Blackshaw Head. About 500m up the hill a hairpin bend to the left is reached but, on the apex of the bend, a farm road (Brown Hill Lane) goes **SA**. Climb steadily up the lane, ignoring footpaths and bridleways off to the right and left respectively. Continue to climb, swinging gently around to the **R** to arrive at a group of renovated houses at Strines Clough Farm at the hilltop lane end.

8 At the end of the first block of buildings turn **R** along a narrow, signposted bridleway, keeping the gardens of other houses on the left. Follow this section of single-track bridleway, crossing two streams and passing through several gates, towards Field Head Farm, nestled among a group of trees to the right. On approaching the farm the grassy track passes ponds and beehives (right), then goes through a gate; keep **SA** over the farm drive.

Pass through another gate on the opposite side of the drive, then follow a grassy path towards a bridlegate. Once through, a steep descent between high banks follows, passing through yet another gate, onto a narrow path that veers to the **L**. The rough track of Sunderland Lane passes above the gardens of Land Farm then swings around to the **R**, all the time keeping to the left of the gardens.

9 The track soon reaches the tarmac surface of School Land Lane, which drops downhill to cross **Colden Water** via a small bridge, and then proceeds to climb steeply to a crossroads with Edge Lane.

Note If in need of provisions a **R** turn along Edge Lane at this junction leads to May's Farm Shop at **High Gate Farm** in less than 300m. At the next small junction turn back sharp **R** into the farmyard and the shop is in a converted barn on the right.

Turn **L** onto Edge Lane, climbing gently past a house (Longtail) on the right. Continue along Edge Lane (still heading uphill) with a high gritstone wall on the left for nearly a mile, to reach a junction of three gates. The two left-hand gates are private farm roads, so take the **RH** gate, which heads out onto open moorland. Looking ahead, follow the route of a line of prominent electricity poles disappearing over the summit of the hill.

⑩ At long last the top of the hill is reached with fine views behind towards Stoodley Pike and Heptonstall Church. Continue along the track (thankfully downhill now), still following the electricity poles, until the Pennine Way joins the PB from the right. Passing through a five-bar gate, the rough track now continues downhill with the cottages at Gorple Lower Reservoir clearly visible at the bottom. Finally, pass through a wrought-iron gate with a horse stile to meet the access track to **Gorple Lower Reservoir** at Gorple Cottages.

⑪ The Pennine Way goes straight across the road at this point but the PB turns **L**, passing Gorple Cottages and onto the reservoir dam. Turn sharp **R** to cross the dam, then **R** again at the other side, following the access road down to Clough Foot parking area (passing the impressive valley of Graining Water across to the right).

On reaching the parking area a gate and horse stile give access onto a tarmac lane (Halifax Road – turn right here for The Pack Horse Inn) leading upwards to the **L**, for just over 1km, to another parking area at **Widdop Reservoir**. The car park is close to the dam wall where gates give access onto a wide causeway across the dam.

⑫ On reaching the other side, turn sharp **R** to run along the southern edge of the reservoir. Passing the Chudders (rock formations) above on the left, and running below a plantation of trees, the trail begins to climb steeply out of the valley. A series of zigzags reaches the point where the Burnley Way footpath joins the PB at a junction of tracks, but continue **SA** here to the top of the climb on the Gorple Gate.

⑬ Ride more easily now as the trail begins to drop downwards, with views to the left of **Gorple Upper Reservoir** and the ruins of abandoned Gorple Farm. Pass between the rocky outcrops of Hare Stones on the left and the Gorple Stones on the right, indicating that you are now leaving Yorkshire and entering Lancashire.

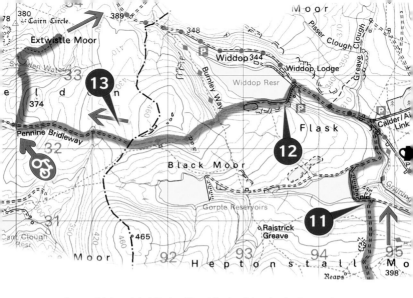

From a high point at Spring Head the track begins to descend more steeply, bearing **L** around the head of Rams Clough. The welcome descent continues to a stream crossing in Smallshaw Clough, before another short climb up the other side provides payback for this downhill fun. At this point watch out for an obvious, newly created bridleway heading off across the bleak moorland to the **R** (signpost and horse stile). This bridleway is the fabled 'Lancashire connection', which leads across Extwistle Moor and on towards the Yorkshire Dales.

Those not intending to head towards the Dales, and wishing to get to Hurstwood from this point, see the map on page 42.
Continue down the Gorple Road for a further 200m, where a wooden farm gate will be met. Don't pass through the gate (signposted *Worsthorne*) but turn **L** immediately in front of it. This is a continuation of the MTL and it drops steadily downhill, alongside the waters of Hurstwood Reservoir on the right.

As the main dam wall is reached, the MTL bears off **L** on the obvious track but a bridlegate at this point leads **SA**, into a copse of trees, on a tarmac path. Follow this pleasant track downhill through the trees until a **L** fork leads over a horse stile and gate into the main parking area of Hurstwood Reservoir.

Section 2

A linear description of the Pennine Bridleway

Climbing towards Boulsworth Dyke on the Brontë Way
(Lancashire Link Part 1)

Tricky riding to the bridge in Turnhole Clough

The Lancashire Link Part 1
Hurstwood to Barnoldswick

START	Hurstwood Reservoir car park **SD 882 312**
FINISH	Road junction with Lister Well Road, Barnoldswick **SD 877 454**
DISTANCE	29km (18 miles)
OFF ROAD	25km (15½ miles)
ON ROAD	4km (2½ miles)
ASCENT	840m (2750ft)
TIME	5–7hrs
MAP	OS Explorer OL21 South Pennines
OVERALL GRADING	■
ACCESS	See Introduction
PUBS	Various in Burnley and Barnoldswick; The Anchor Inn, Salterforth
CAFÉS	Various in Burnley and Barnoldswick; Wycoller Tea Shop, Wycoller Country Park

On the eastern fringes of Burnley lie the villages of Worsthorne and Hurstwood. Between these two hamlets, Hurstwood Reservoir can be found tucked snugly into its moorland setting. Hurstwood has no particular claim to fame, other than it happens to be situated at one of the most northerly points on the Mary Towneley Loop. This geographical quirk means that Hurstwood provides a convenient setting-off point for the next stage of the route across the moors towards Long Preston and the Yorkshire section of the Pennine Bridleway.

map continues on p46

Directions

1 **Hurstwood** village is effectively a cul-de-sac where the tarmac road ends at a junction of gravel tracks immediately in front of a telephone box. The right-hand track quickly turns a corner to the left and opens up into a sizeable parking area, popular with walkers, dog owners and cyclists. Numerous signs and information boards indicate that the PB runs alongside the westernmost edge of the car park, where a choice of gates or stiles gives access to a tarmac track running through woodland.

The PB follows the track uphill towards the dam area of **Hurstwood Reservoir**. The wooded section gives way to open moorland as the dam wall is met at a junction of tracks. Follow the signposted trail, which climbs gently alongside the eastern shore of the reservoir. For a short time now the route follows the Mary Towneley Loop in a clockwise direction.

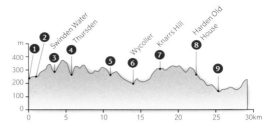

The trail climbs steadily, following the wide, gravel track (with the water to the left) past the end of the reservoir to an obvious T-junction of tracks just outside the village of Worsthorne. This is the Gorple Road; turn **R** and head **E** across the moor for about 200m to where the start of a newly created bridleway will be found **L**.

Note This well-surfaced trail will not appear on older OS maps because it has only been in existence since 2009 and was created specifically to carry the PB northwards, towards the Forest of Trawden.

2 Leave the Mary Towneley Loop at this point (the end of the Summit to Hurstwood section described earlier) by turning **L** onto the bridleway and head off **N** across **Extwistle Moor**. After a gentle rise, the deep valley of the **Swinden Water** leading towards Swinden Reservoir will be met.

3 Here the trail zigzags down the hillside around some particularly acute hairpin bends (berms), before crossing the stream and climbing in a similar fashion up

Downhill to Swinden Water – but then comes the payback!

the other side. More uphill riding, on a good trail, eventually leads to a junction with a footpath coming in left from Swinden Reservoir. Keep **R** here (signposted *PB*) and continue along to a gate on the moor top. Here the trail turns sharp **L** in front of the gate and begins an exciting descent towards a junction of roads above the hamlet of **Thursden**. The descent is steep, rocky and entertaining as more bermed hairpins are encountered.

Eventually the trail exits onto tarmac just above two **cattle grids**: one road drops straight ahead and the other (the official route) descends steeply to the **L**. Either of these roads can be taken; the direct road (**SA**) drops steeply to cross Thursden Brook and then climbs, just as steeply, up the other side of the hill. Alternatively the **LH** road can be taken; this also descends steeply, but the PB then enters woodland on the right-hand side of the road, just **before** the bridge over Thursden Brook (watch out for the **PB sign**). Once in the wood the trail climbs steeply uphill, eventually leaving the trees and meeting the road again (at the top of the direct climb taken by those following the tarmac route).

4 A short way further along the road turns sharp left but, immediately before this bend, an obvious trail will be seen going off **R** (the next section of bridleway). Older maps will show this section of track as footpath, but it

The bridge over Turnhole Clough (photo: Steve Bramall)

has now been officially re-designated as bridleway so can be ridden across the corner of **Red Spa Moor** to pick up the excellent farm track carrying the Brontë Way (passing an intriguing arch, which is all that remains of New House Farm) then on towards the farm at **Boulsworth Dyke**.

Around 800m beyond Boulsworth Dyke the farm track bears off sharp left, but on the junction a signpost indicates that the bridleway continues **SA**, up a short rise. **The ongoing grassy surface is badly eroded in places** but is rideable with care, until it curves gently around to the left (**N**) and begins to descend more steeply along the left-hand bank of a steep-sided valley. The continuation of the descent, to a bridge across Turnhole Clough, is **steep and tricky to ride in places**, but the path becomes much easier after the bridge has been crossed.

5 A short climb below the farm at **Brink Ends** leads to much easier riding as the Brontë Way is followed to a junction of trails about 800m beyond the bridge. The approach to this junction is up a short, steep rise, and at the top a sharp **L** turn through a gate indicates the way ahead, dropping steeply downhill towards Wycoller Country Park. **Wycoller** is in a beautiful setting and provides a visitor centre, café and picnic spots galore.

The approach to the village will keep the stream on the left, passing a number of ancient bridges on the way. The first buildings met are the visitor centre (with toilets) and immediately beyond will be found the remains of the original hall, now sadly in ruins. Opposite the old hall is a clapper (slab) bridge, which can be used as an alternative crossing to the slippery ford a few metres further down the lane. If neither of these crossing points is to your liking, a further bridge with a most peculiar, misshapen arch can be used as a final crossing point before the tea shop is reached.

The tarmac lane now leaves the stream for a short distance, passing between the tea shop (a pit stop here is highly recommended for a quick energy boost because the route out of Wycoller will be decidedly upwards in nature!) and some attractively restored farmhouses.

6 From the tea shop follow the lane through the village for a short distance until it turns sharp **L** and crosses the stream again. **Immediately** over the bridge, take a **R** turn into an unsurfaced lane that runs between the stream on the right and houses on the left (also the route of the Pendle Way footpath).

The lane quickly crosses the stream again and, after a few more metres, a new track goes off **R**, through a gate, heading ominously upwards (another gate a little way along the lane leads to the 'pump house', with a

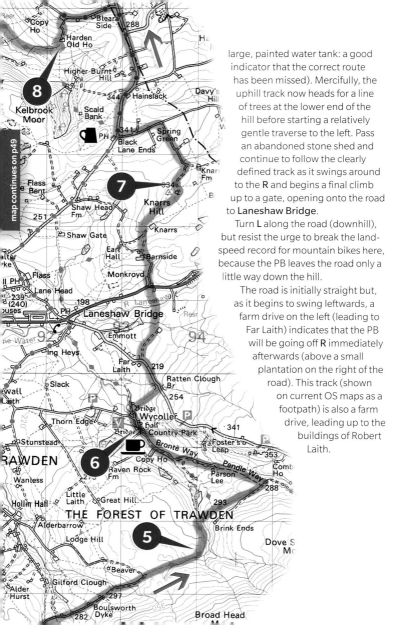

map continues on p49

large, painted water tank: a good indicator that the correct route has been missed). Mercifully, the uphill track now heads for a line of trees at the lower end of the hill before starting a relatively gentle traverse to the left. Pass an abandoned stone shed and continue to follow the clearly defined track as it swings around to the **R** and begins a final climb up to a gate, opening onto the road to **Laneshaw Bridge**.

Turn **L** along the road (downhill), but resist the urge to break the land-speed record for mountain bikes here, because the PB leaves the road only a little way down the hill.

The road is initially straight but, as it begins to swing leftwards, a farm drive on the left (leading to Far Laith) indicates that the PB will be going off **R** immediately afterwards (above a small plantation on the right of the road). This track (shown on current OS maps as a footpath) is also a farm drive, leading up to the buildings of Robert Laith.

Easy trails and fine descents

Note The next few miles of the PB utilise footpaths recently upgraded to bridleway status to avoid some busy sections of road en route to the public house at **Black Lane Ends**.

On reaching the farm buildings of Robert Laith, turn **L** immediately – alongside the first garden – to pass through a gate and follow the obvious track across the field ahead. The track soon turns sharp **R** to cross Hullown Beck then climbs briefly out of the hollow, keeping to the left of a wooden electricity pole, to continue onto the deeply incised streamway of the **River Laneshaw**. Cross the river on a new bridge then climb briefly up a small rise between two ancient hawthorn bushes. Keeping to the left of the boundary wall, follow it out to meet the **A6068** directly opposite the small hamlet of **Monkroyd**.

Crossing the road with care, follow the narrow tarmac lane as it climbs steeply up the hill towards the farm at **Barnside**. Just beyond Barnside, a muddy farm track heads off left towards Earl Hall but ignore this, continuing up the tarmac lane until it meets a cattle grid at a wall. Immediately before the cattle grid, however, a new track keeps to the left of the wall, leading up to a wooden farm gate. Once through the gate, the very obvious gravel track continues straight ahead up to the brow of **Knarrs Hill**.

7 Once on the top, a gate will be found on the **R**, leading through into the next field. A long, straight section of newly laid track then follows, until a short dogleg leads through yet another gate into the next field.

The track now traverses a sunken area of broken ground, below a white-painted trig point, climbing briefly up to follow a continuation of the boundary wall a little further along. The track now begins to drop downhill, joining a much older farm lane where it crosses a cattle grid, and begins to drop more steeply through a patch of woodland.

After a number of sharp bends, the roughly surfaced lane begins a long, arrow-straight climb, passing the entrance drive to Hazelgrove Lodge and continuing up to a junction with Warley Wise Lane. The worst of the climb is now over as a **L** turn along Warley Wise Lane leads up to another junction, this time with a much busier road, just above the Black Lane Ends public house.

> **Note** The next section of the PB is planned to go cross-country between Warley Wise Lane and Harden Old House on Bleara Road. Unfortunately, at the time of writing, this short section of route does not have the legal permissions in place and, because of funding cut-backs, it is likely to be some considerable time before these are successfully processed. Until these legal niceties can be completed a 3.2km diversion on road is necessary, but the good news is that most of it is downhill!

From the junction just above the pub, take a **R** turn and continue to climb a little further to the top of the hill at **Hainslack** (where the official PB will eventually cross the road as it climbs over Burnt Hill towards Kitchen). Follow the main road to the **L**, dropping steeply downhill before climbing again to a road junction on the **L** that leads to Earby (Bleara Road).

Follow this quiet road, passing entrances to farms at **Bleara Side** and Out Laithe. Immediately before the farm buildings at Cocket a signposted bridleway drops downhill to the left towards **Harden Old House**.

8 Turn **L** down this drive, but immediately in front of the main gates to Harden Old House take the vague track to the **L**. This then swings back **R**, around the edge of the garden and through one farm gate, then **R** again to run along the bottom of the garden and through another gate into a large, muddy field alongside a small stream.

Note At this point a vague footpath will be found joining the bridleway from the south. This is where the official route of the PB will re-join the interim (road-based) route.

The next few fields are boggy and hard to ride with a less-clearly defined track. At each field boundary look carefully for the exit gate through the fence on the opposite side of the field.

Eventually, a final farm gate leads into a lane giving much easier riding down towards Heads House. A short distance beyond the buildings at Heads House an unsurfaced lane (with PB fingerpost) will be found going off to the **R**. Turn into this lane and follow it up to a junction with a farm gate. At this point a narrow section of single-track will be found heading off under a shady lane to the **R**. This short section quickly passes through a farm gate into open fields, where another gate will be found immediately beyond the prominent electricity pole in the corner just ahead. A **L** turn through this gate gives access to the adjoining field. Head directly across

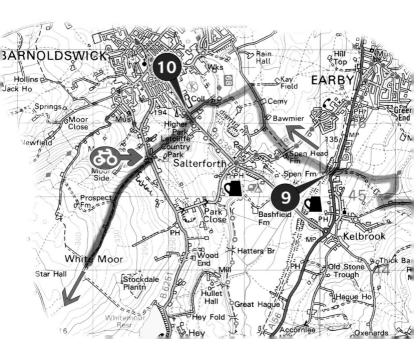

An evening ride through Wycoller Country Park

the centre, with no defined path, aiming immediately to the right of the largest tree on the far side.

On passing this large tree, the gate on the other side of the field will become evident. The bridleway passes through this before turning immediately sharp **L**. The next field gate is just ahead at this point; once through it turn half-**L**, heading across the field and aiming for the roofline of some prominent industrial buildings. A series of wooden posts marks the start of an obvious, raised trackway, heading towards the same buildings, where yet another gate opens onto a farm track leading down into the village of Sough.

At the bottom of the farm drive, immediately before a cattle grid, a signposted gate gives access to a narrow lane running alongside factory buildings on the right. The lane quickly meets a main road, where a staggered crossing (**L** then **R**) leads under a disused railway and through a gate into a large field.

9 There is no obvious track across this field but a diagonal route towards the high bank in the top corner leads to a small marker post. A steep climb up the hill alongside the boundary fence guided by a PB guidepost then leads to a gate into a narrow lane. This lane goes off sharp **L**, then bears around to the **R**, to a group of cottages. Ignore the main tarmac lane going off right here (the drive to a house) and take the less-obvious route **SA**, past the front doors of the cottages and out to a quiet lane. Crossing straight over this road, a continuation of the bridleway will be found, which runs under the shade of the trees to another quiet road with a prominent milestone (containing evidence of an early example of misspelled stonemasonry) in the opposite verge. Turn **R** up this tarmac lane, which soon passes a cemetery on the right. Ignoring the entrance drive to Far Hey Farm, continue a short distance further to where the tarmac surface ends, and find an obvious, double-gated entrance to a bridleway on the **L**.

   The track now follows the boundary wall and fence on the left down an exhilaratingly steep hill to another gate leading out to a tarmac track. Cross the Leeds and Liverpool Canal (via Cockshott Bridge) alongside a small marina, where a **R** turn leads along a gravel track. A short distance further the track turns sharp **L** to run alongside the playing fields of West Craven Technology College and out to the busy **B6383**.

10 Turn **L** for a few metres then carefully cross the road, where a track heads off sharply uphill on a cobbled surface to farm gate leading into the open fields of Salterforth Country Park. A few yards into the field the farm track forks. Take the **LH** track (the lower one) across the field (Hurst Hill), then alongside a hedge. Continue along the clearly defined track, which soon becomes a tarmac lane as it passes Bleak House and climbs gently to meet the **B6251** at a T-junction. A **L** turn here climbs briefly up to a junction with Lister Well Road and the continuation of the PB towards the Dales.

Clocking up a few miles on traffic-free lanes

The Lancashire Link Part 2
Barnoldswick to Long Preston

START	Road junction with Lister Well Road, Barnoldswick **SD 877 454**
FINISH	Village green, Long Preston **SD 834 582**
DISTANCE	24km (15 miles)
OFF ROAD	14km (8¾ miles)
ON ROAD	10km (6¼ miles)
ASCENT	390m (1270ft)
TIME	3–5hrs
MAP	OS Explorer OL41 Forest of Bowland & Ribblesdale
OVERALL GRADING	■
PUBS	Various in Barnoldswick; The Buck Inn, Paythorne; Maypole Inn and The Boars Head Hotel, Long Preston
CAFÉS	Various in Barnoldswick; The Naked Man Café, Settle

60% OFF ROAD

One tough climb away from Barnoldswick, then easier terrain follows! The ascent of White Moor is the final sting in the tail as the Pennine Bridleway heads into the pastoral farmland beyond. Easy riding through Gisburn and Paythorne leads towards the River Ribble and the official entry of the route into Yorkshire (it has already strayed briefly into and out of the county on a couple of occasions in previous sections).

From **Barnoldswick** town centre the **B6251** quickly begins its climb up towards Whitemoor Reservoir. As the last few houses of the town are passed, a disused quarry on the right of the road is met, and at this point a narrow tarmac lane also goes off uphill to the right. This is Lister Well Road and the junction is signposted to indicate that it is also a bridleway – the next section of the Pennine Bridleway – that climbs steadily across the flanks of White Moor. If starting the ride from this

point, plenty of suitable road-
side parking will be found in
the area.

DIRECTIONS

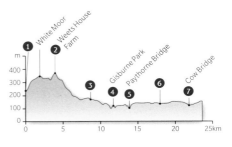

1 The climb up
White Moor could be
described as a 'steady
trog', meaning (in this
case) 'not too steep
– but long and painful'. Initially the climbing is on tarmac, but beyond
Prospect Farm the lane becomes unsurfaced, providing a sandy trail with
the odd rocky section to add interest. Eventually tarmac is
reached on the very quiet Gisburn Old
Road, high above Barrowford. A
R turn along the

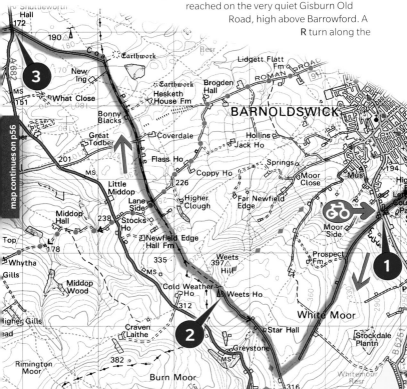

map continues on p56

road soon descends past **Star Hall** before climbing steeply back up to reach the end of the tarmac at **Weets House Farm**.

Rocky riding across the Level of Weets

2 Pass through the gate, looking for the only track heading downwards, marking the start of **a long and furious descent**. The first downhill section, across the Level of Weets, is eroded, making for some tricky riding in places. Eventually a farm gate is reached, giving access to a much easier riding surface that continues splendidly downhill, passing drives to farms at Lane Side, Coverdale and Bonny Blacks. From the farm at **Bonny Blacks** the lane is surfaced with tarmac (Coal Pit Lane), which swings sharp **L** then continues to meet the **A682**, 800m south of Gisburn.

3 Directly across the **A682** is the drive to **Westby Hall Farm**. Continue down the drive and into the farmyard, where a sharp **R** turn around the last barn leads onto a continuation of the bridleway. Entering a large field, the route is not easy to follow (or ride) but it essentially keeps close to the left-hand boundary and runs quickly down to a junction with the very busy **A59**.

Continue **SA** across the main road into another field directly opposite. The track across this field is much easier to spot and follows the right-hand field boundary until, approaching the far end, a diagonal route **L** heads for a gate, allowing access onto a bridge over the railway. More easy track, and a further gate, leads into the yard of Coppice Farm where a **L** turn gives access towards a tarmac drive. Just before the drive is reached, however, take a narrow signposted path on the **R** to reach the farm drive just beyond a cattle grid. The drive is then followed to the **R** to meet a B road at Mill Lane.

4 Turn **L** along Mill Lane, dropping steeply down through Coppice Wood, to meet the **River Ribble** at Gisburn Bridge. Immediately before the bridge turn **R** on a bridleway, which climbs steeply up through the wood on a tarmac surface before emerging into the open at an attractive viewpoint overlooking Gisburn Park and the old Hall (currently a hospital).

Continue along the top edge of a paddock in front of the Hall to a junction of roads at the far end. Follow a narrow road **SA** into the trees before dropping steeply down to cross a bridge over Stock Beck. Beyond the bridge the tarmac is replaced by a good, hard-packed surface; climb back up through the wood, behind the houses and barns. At the top of the climb the track swings to the **R**, heads out across fields and, shortly afterwards, arrives at a junction with the **A682**.

To avoid riding along this unpleasantly busy road a dedicated bridleway has been created to take the more refined PB traffic. This new track runs by the road, through fields, before briefly running alongside the road again. When the road bends sharp right the track continues due **N** across Castle Haugh Hill on an existing bridleway. Continue heading diagonally across the next field, past the historic remains of **Castle Haugh**, and through a small wood to exit onto a road by **Paythorne Bridge**.

5 River crossings always tend to be the lowest point in any landscape setting and Paythorne Bridge is no exception. Cross the bridge and begin the long, slow trudge, out of the valley bottom and up into the village of **Paythorne**. A small chapel on the left of the road is one of the first buildings met, and

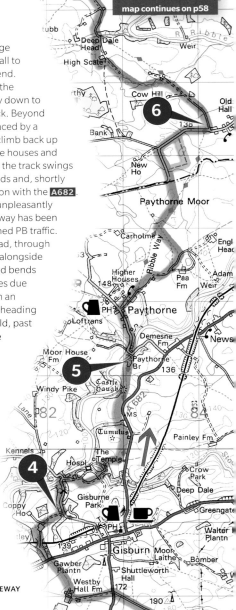

directly opposite a signposted bridleway heads off along the intriguingly named Paa Lane.

Pass a farm on the right and, a little further along, cross Dodgson Gill. Now continue along a particularly straight section of lane until a cattle grid is reached by a barn. Immediately before the cattle grid, a lane turns off **L** to join up with a track, Ing Lane. Ing Lane is shown as a footpath on older maps but has now been redesignated as bridleway so it can be ridden with full legal status.

After a short distance, a sharp **R** turn leads to a continuation of the lane, which is followed easily across **Paythorne Moor**. At a junction of tracks take the **L** branch, which runs between fences, bearing first **L**, then **R**, and finally passes through a gate into a large open field. From here the track is easily followed diagonally across the field to exit onto a road, on the apex of a sharp bend, a little to the south of Ged Beck Bridge. From here there is a choice of routes.

Don't forget to shut the gate!

Either follow the road **N**, crossing Ged Beck Bridge, and up to a junction with Long Bank Lane. A sharp **R** turn then leads on towards the village of Halton West.

Alternatively (a tougher option), immediately beyond Ged Bridge a gate allows access into a field on the **R** of the road. Cross the first field and half the second, where a line of gnarled trees marks the line of an ancient field boundary, now fallen into disrepair. The bridleway (not shown on current OS maps) runs immediately alongside this row of trees but there is no defined path and, if the grass has not recently been cut, the riding will be correspondingly strenuous. The bridleway continues to follow the line of trees into another field, where the riding becomes easier as a track is met, leading to the road just west of Halton West. A **R** turn here joins the easier road route, which continues towards the village.

If you are interested in a little extra-curricular activity, a number of specialist bike trails in Gisburn Forest Park can be accessed from the trail centre at Cocklet Hill car park or from Gisburn Forest Bikes at Tosside. Both venues can be accessed from Halton West or Wigglesworth via a 6–8km detour from the main trail. Visit www.gisburnforestbikes.co.uk for more details.

6 Pay attention as the first farm buildings of Halton West are reached and watch out for a bridleway going off **L**, just in front of the buildings (helpfully indicated by a large boulder on the side of the road). This unsurfaced farm track (Brook Lane) leads the way onwards towards a well-earned rest at Long Preston. Follow the excellent smooth, gravel surface of Brook Lane, keeping **SA** at a junction where a farm drive goes off left. A short distance further along, the boundary fence of Low Scale Farm is approached. Immediately on the **L** at this point is a newly constructed gate, giving access to a diverted section of bridleway avoiding the farmyard.

Once into the field, the new route across is not easy to locate but aim generally for the prominent telecommunications mast on the far horizon. A stream crosses the field before a line of telegraph poles is reached, but a small, inconspicuous bridge enables this to be crossed with dry feet (look carefully for it if the field is planted with crops). Maintain the same direction until a fence corner to the **R** provides a suitable landmark. From this corner a farm gate can be seen a little way over to the **L**, leading to easier terrain.

Through the gate, an indistinct track leads towards the farm buildings of **High Scale Farm**, but once again the bridleway has been diverted to avoid the farmyard. As the farm boundary is approached bear **L**, then **R**, around the top of barns, where more

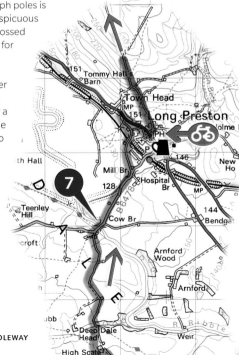

obvious paths all lead into a narrow, sunken track running alongside the boundary fence. Follow this track, away from the farm buildings, to the top corner of the field, where a signposted bridleway gate leads into the adjoining field.

Sweet single-track en route to Long Preston

A few metres ahead, another bridleway gate gives access to a large field, where a diagonal route **L** (follow the direction of the fingerpost across the field, gently downhill to the opposite corner) leads out through another gate onto the main farm drive. Turn **L**, crossing a bridge over Deep Dale Syke before following Todmanhaw Lane past numerous farms and houses to meet the **B6478** at **Cow Bridge End**.

7 A **R** turn along the **B6478** quickly crosses the **River Ribble** again; the road then begins to climb gently up towards Long Preston. Before the buildings of the village are reached, a small bridge zigzags first **L** then **R** over a stream. Immediately beyond the bridge, Back Lane goes off **L**, a much quieter approach into **Long Preston**.

The lane runs alongside gardens on the right, then past two or three houses on its left-hand side. The Pennine Bridleway team are currently negotiating a more direct route into the centre of the village from this point but, until an alternative route gains legal approval, continue to follow Back Lane a little further, where it will be found to take a sharp **R** turn and climb gently up to a junction with the very busy **A65**. This interim route then takes a **R** turn along the main road, which leads to a Pelican crossing and the main village green after a short distance.

Climbing up from Long Preston towards Hunter Bark (photo: Geoff Cater)

The Yorkshire Dales Part 1
Long Preston to Horton-in-Ribblesdale

START	Village green, Long Preston **SD 834 582**
FINISH	Crown Hotel, Horton-in-Ribblesdale **SD 808 726**
DISTANCE	37km (23 miles)
OFF ROAD	24km (15 miles)
ON ROAD	13km (8 miles)
ASCENT	980m (3200ft)
TIME	7–9hrs
MAPS	OS Explorers OL41 Forest of Bowland & Ribblesdale, OL2 Yorkshire Dales (Southern & Western areas)
OVERALL GRADING	■
ACCESS	See Introduction
PUBS	Craven Heifer, Stainforth; The Game Cock Inn, Austwick; Crown Hotel and The Golden Lion Hotel (bunkhouse), Horton-in-Ribblesdale
CAFÉS	Elaine's Tearooms, Feizor; The Pen-y-ghent Café and Blind Beck Tearooms, Horton-in-Ribblesdale

65%
OFF ROAD

Welcome to the Yorkshire Dales at their finest! The route from Long Preston to Horton-in-Ribblesdale leads through some of the most spectacular limestone scenery in Britain. Grassy trails, limestone pavement and rocky tracks are the order of the day, with a couple of steep climbs to clear the lungs and get the heart pumping. Facilities are never very far away on this section, with short detours giving access to traditional Dales villages along the route. The following section over to Ribblehead and Garsdale will have a very different feel, so stock up on essential supplies in advance.

map continues on p65

DIRECTIONS

1 Face the Maypole
Inn on the village
green and turn **R**,
then first **L** to enter
Green Gate Lane,
which climbs steeply
out of the village. After
800m a lane joins the
road from the left, which
may cause a little confusion:
currently a *PB* signpost points
back down the hill towards
Long Preston. This lane was
intended to be the preferred
route before it was changed to the
current option of Green Gate Lane.
Ignore this signpost and continue
to struggle up the hill (which at
some point becomes Edge Lane); the
gradient gradually eases as the top is
approached.

    The tarmac eventually runs out at a
large grassy, parking/turning area, but
the lane continues as a roughly surfaced
farm track.

2 Easy riding, with an occasional steeper
section, climbs past the disused quarries
of **Hunter Bark** before a welcome
downhill section towards the trees of
Black's Plantation. A quick breather
approaching this highpoint gives a
chance to enjoy splendid all-round
views. Ahead are the unmistakable
outlines of Ingleborough and Attermire
Scar, while to the south is the impressive
bulk of Pendle Hill, highlighting the route
the PB has taken to reach this point.

A brief section of track between trees leads to a junction with a bridleway coming up from the left (from Lodge Farm) but ignore this by bearing **R** at the junction to meet another junction a few yards further on.

Note The tarmac lane to the left here is Mitchell Lane, which leads **L** downhill to Settle. An alternative route (the Settle Loop) leads off **R** from this junction and is highly recommended (route description continues from point **2** on page 97). If you intend to visit the town before tackling the Settle Loop, bear in mind that the painful 170m-plus climb from Long Preston will have to be repeated from the opposite side of Settle when your visit is over.

To continue on the PB turn **L** down Mitchell Lane, which quickly steepens to give an exhilarating run, passing the first houses of Upper Settle and reaching a road junction. Keep **L** (downhill) at the junction and follow the road into the Market Square (Tourist Information Centre at the southern end).

3 After a (possible) break pick up the PB again from the TIC. With your back to the building turn **L** and go up a

The start of Lambert Lane on the Settle Loop (photo: Steve Bramall)

short distance to a junction with High Street (not to be confused with the main road through town, Duke Street). Turn **L** along High Street and follow it to the far end of the Market Square where a narrow lane goes off **R** and steeply uphill (Constitution Hill) to climb towards Castlebergh Plantation. Ignore the lane off to the right (which drops back down into town) and follow the road as it turns sharp **L**, still climbing, to a Y-junction with a signposted bridleway leading off **R**. The gravel-surfaced bridleway continues to climb steeply but gives an excellent riding surface, with prominent drainage humps, before eventually meeting a gate by an old ruined barn.

Great riding on a classic Yorkshire drove road (photo: Geoff Cater)

Pass through the gate onto a grassy track, which climbs (more gently now) up to another farm gate, leading into a short section of walled lane. The field soon opens out again but the track continues by the wall on the left, towards a small copse a little way ahead, with lovely views left over Settle and Giggleswick. More grassy track passes a ladder stile then climbs a small rise to a gate into a large field, which slopes down to a wooded area on the left. At this point, the trail climbs uphill and diagonally **R** to encounter a short, rocky embankment, which may well require a dismount and push.

The single-track bridleway now traverses leftwards around the hillside (still gently climbing) up to a gate by a copse. Once through the gate, a further short climb leads to yet another gate, followed by a short descent and climb across a dry gully, then a continuation of the traverse. The single-track bridleway eventually encounters a gate, leading onto a quiet tarmac road. To the left the road drops very steeply into Langcliffe but the PB goes off **R**, uphill again, along the quiet, attractive road to Cowside and Henside.

Note A bridleway will soon be passed, coming steeply down from a double farm gate on the right. This is the Settle Loop, and both routes now rejoin.

After 800m a narrow, tarmac lane goes off **L**, just beyond a cattle grid, to a group of farms at **Upper Winskill** (signposted *PB*). Follow this lane as far as the main farm entrance to find an initially bewildering array of five gates. The rightmost gate is signposted as belonging to Upper Winskill, where an obvious (signposted) bridleway will be found going **R**, by a wall, above the farm buildings.

4 A little way along this farm track a short section of walled lane is entered, leading into the next field. Follow the track across the middle of the field until it splits almost directly opposite a large barn on the left. Take the less well-defined track to the **L** here as it heads across to join the field wall again.

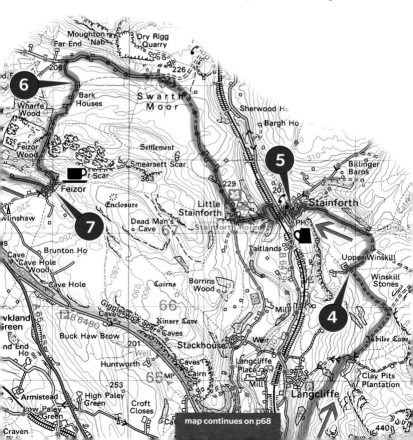

map continues on p68

Classic Dales scenery

After about 100m the bridleway meets an unsurfaced lane just above a gate, signposted *PB to Stainforth*. Pass through the gate and follow the lane downhill **L** to another gate immediately above the impressive waterfall of **Catrigg Force**. Once through this gate the track becomes a walled lane, running delightfully downhill alongside Stainforth Beck. **Show a little caution on this descent** because the lane is narrow and very popular with walkers heading up from Stainforth to visit Catrigg Force. After a fun-filled, rocky descent, the lane meets tarmac again in **Stainforth** village where refreshments can be found in the popular hostelry the Craven Heifer, in a delightful situation by Stainforth Beck.

5 Turn sharp **L** where the rocky bridleway meets tarmac. A short distance down this lane, a **R** turn leads directly to the front of the Craven Heifer where another **R** turn indicates the correct direction to take upon leaving said hostelry!

Cross the bridge over the beck (travelling away from the pub) and take a **L** turn to quickly meet the busy **B6479** at a T-junction. Do not go out onto the main road; immediately before the junction there is a car park (with toilets) on the **L**. Head diagonally across this to the bottom corner nearest the river, where an underpass leads under the **B6479** and into a grassy picnic area. **Note that signposts at each end of the underpass request that riders dismount.** Mounting blocks have been provided at each end for equestrian use.

A new bridleway now runs up the side and along the top edge of the picnic area and leads out, through a gate, onto a farm lane. Turn **L** up the lane, which climbs gently before ending at two farm gates, side by side. Don't pass through either gate: turn **R** on a newly constructed section of bridleway, which runs above the railway line before exiting onto tarmac next to the railway bridge at Dog Hill Brow.

The PB now turns **L** along the road; dropping steeply downhill to cross the River Ribble in a very attractive situation, before climbing just as steeply back up, and continuing alongside a caravan park into the village of **Little Stainforth**. Once in the village take a **RH** turn at a crossroads onto a minor road heading **N** towards Hargreaves Barn and Banks Barn. A little further along, the road runs across more open countryside without the usual boundary of drystone walling; shortly after the impressive quarry complex (**Dry Rigg Quarry**) at Helwith Bridge begins to draw in view.

A short descent leads to a junction with the Helwith Bridge-to-Austwick road where a **L** turn is required. Less than 500m later a signposted bridleway will be found on the left. This bridleway has been recently resurfaced and, once down the initial short hill from the road, it turns sharp **R**, through a farm gate, to follow the line of electricity poles across the field ahead.

6 At the other side of the field a farm gate leads into an unsurfaced lane, which in turn climbs up to the rear of the farm buildings of Lower Bark House. Do not pass through the gate into the farmyard, but bear **L** along the farm track leading gently uphill towards Higher Bark House and **Wharfe Wood**. Once past Higher Bark House, a gate is encountered; once through this the track remains easy to follow as it climbs steadily to another gate approaching the top of the hill. Beyond the summit gate an attractive lane descends, gently at first and then more steeply, into the hamlet of **Feizor**.

7 A gate leads onto the tarmac road running through the village (café). Follow this road until it crosses a cobbled ford (often dry), then just on the next bend turn **R** along a signposted bridleway between farm buildings (Hale Lane). Initially the track has a concrete surface but soon becomes rockier as the farm buildings are left behind. Excellent riding now follows along a good walled track until a T-junction is reached at a partially ruined barn (Meldings Barn).

Turn **R** at the barn, along another similar track, to run below **Oxenber Wood** (right). More fantastic riding leads, after about 800m, to a junction of four bridleways. The PB runs **SA**, dropping downhill again to a substantial ford across Austwick Beck, with a convenient slab bridge to the left (Flascoe Bridge). Once across the beck follow the continuation of the lane, to meet the Austwick-to-Wharfe road again on the outskirts of **Austwick**.

> **Note** Turn **L** to visit the village, which has a very pleasant pub (The Game Cock Inn) serving excellent meals and offering accommodation. There is also a shop/Post Office where dwindling supplies can be replenished.

map continues on p70

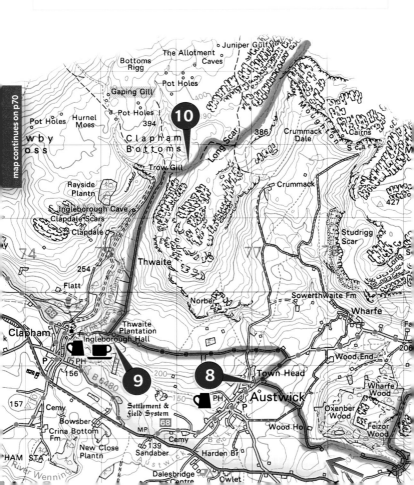

8 Turn **R** at the junction, heading away from Austwick along the road towards Wharfe. About 400m later (but before reaching Wharfe) a signposted bridleway will be found on the **L**; follow this to where the rocky

Austwick village (photo: EA Bowness)

lane turns sharp **L** alongside Slaindale Barn. The bridleway now begins to climb steeply until, approaching the top of the hill, a junction with a quiet road (Crummack Lane) is met. **SA** at this junction is the obvious track of Thwaite Lane, which, following extensive regrading, gives an excellent riding surface as it climbs steadily past Long Tram Plantation (left). The riding along Thwaite Lane becomes easier now, with fine views to Norber and Crummack Dale to the right. After about 2.5km of very pleasant riding a large plantation is met as Thwaite Lane begins its rocky descent into **Clapham** village.

Note To visit Clapham keep **SA** steeply down the lane, passing through two disconcertingly dark tunnels on the way. Clapham is another very attractive village with all necessary facilities including a shop, pubs, cafés, a small outdoor shop and the local headquarters of the Cave and Fell Rescue Service.

9 If not wishing to visit Clapham, at the plantation turn **R** on Long Lane, which drops steeply before beginning a long, steady ascent, high above the popular tourist attractions of Clapdale Drive and **Ingleborough Cave**. Long Lane eventually levels out, and even drops downhill a little, before beginning its final steep, rocky climb, up to a farm gate opening leading onto open, grassy, fellside. Once through the track is easy to spot as it climbs diagonally **R** up to another gate.

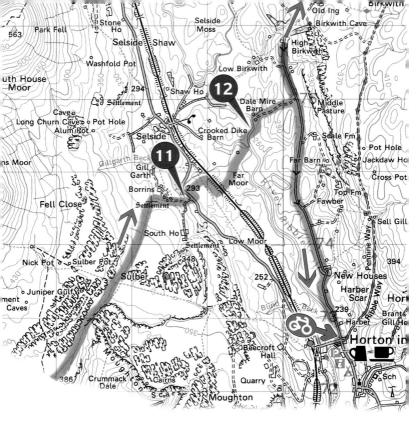

10 Continue through the gate to the next wall corner, where the track divides and a little confusion may occur. Both tracks soon meet up again on the top of the hill, but the lower, **LH** track gives the easier path through **Long Scar** and up to a junction of tracks on the summit plateau a little way ahead. Both tracks emerge onto a much larger, obvious one running **N** towards Sulber Gate. A couple of paths branching off this main track drop down the hill to the right, whereas the PB track keeps level as it runs across the flatter top of the plateau.

This section of the trail has suffered some erosion from the passage of motorised vehicles but recent bans have enabled a certain amount of recovery, and the route now follows a lovely grassy trail through the superb limestone scenery of Sulber Gate. Shortly, a junction of paths is met at a gate just above Sulber Nick. This gate marks the start of a well-earned descent into Ribblesdale, so enjoy the ride as the trail eventually turns sharp **R** near **Borrins Farm**, before dropping to meet the `B6479` a little below the hamlet of Selside.

11 Cross the road here, and immediately turn **L** (towards Selside) along a newly built path alongside the road. After a few metres a bridleway gate gives access onto a newly created track running down the hill to the **R**. This new bridleway (not shown on current maps) passes through two farm gates then winds round to the **R** to a tunnel under the railway.

12 Once on the other side the trail continues to descend across **Far Moor** to an impressive, new, equine-friendly bridge over the **River Ribble**. The bridleway then turns **L**, alongside the river, to meet an access track at Dale Mire Barn. This farm track is then followed steeply uphill to the **R** to meet a very quiet tarmac road leading from Horton up to farms at High Birkwith. The PB turns **L** here to climb steadily up to High Birkwith Farm in about 1.2km. Alternatively, a **R** turn at this point will follow the lane downhill,

The new bridge over the Ribble at Selside (photo: Nick Crosby)

through the very small hamlet of **New Houses** (no facilities) and down into **Horton-in-Ribblesdale** about 800m further on.

Note If a visit to **Horton-in-Ribblesdale** is planned the route will have to be reversed to return to this point to continue on the PB. Horton is a busy village: facilities include a couple of pubs (one with a bunkhouse), a campsite, general store and an excellent café/outdoor shop.

Heading for Sulber Nick with Pen-y-ghent in the distance

The Yorkshire Dales Part 2
Horton-in-Ribblesdale to Garsdale Head

START	Crown Hotel, Horton-in-Ribblesdale **SD 808 726**
FINISH	Moorcock Inn, Garsdale Head **SD 797 927**
DISTANCE	28.25km (17½ miles)
OFF ROAD	18.75km (11½ miles)
ON ROAD	9.5km (6 miles)
ASCENT	760m (2500ft)
TIME	4hrs 30mins–6hrs 30mins
MAPS	OS Explorers OL2 Yorkshire Dales (Southern & Western areas), OL19 Howgill Fells & Upper Eden Valley
OVERALL GRADING	■
PUBS	Moorcock Inn, Garsdale Head
CAFÉS	None on route

65%
OFF ROAD

If the previous section of the Pennine Bridleway were to be defined as 'Dales and villages', this section could be more properly described as 'remote upland'. Today there will be no villages, no shops, sadly not even a pub, without a detour for a couple of miles to The Station Inn at Ribblehead. An alternative name for today's trek could be 'The Settle-to-Carlisle link', because the Settle–Carlisle railway will be your regular companion. In case of mishap the most convenient escape route would be via the stations at Ribblehead or Dent.

To reach the starting point, head to the northern end of the village, where the road crosses one bridge then begins to turn sharp **L** over another. The Crown Hotel is situated between these two bridges, where a very quiet lane will be found between the river and the pub.

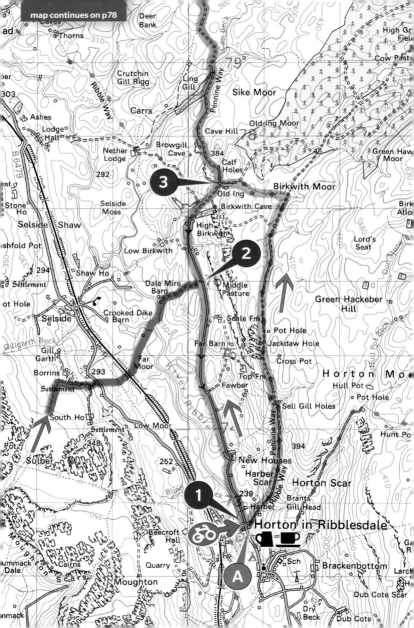

map continues on p78

Directions

1 Follow the lane up to the junction with the PB (the end of the Long Preston to Horton-in-Ribblesdale section).

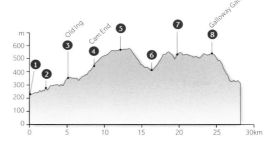

2 Continue along the lane, climbing steadily up to **High Birkwith Farm** in about 1 km where the tarmac surface ends at a gate by the farmyard. Pass through and climb the rocky hill ahead, passing (and ignoring) a junction with a farm track off to the right. A little further up the hill, the farm at **Old Ing** will be found on the right, and another gate is met.

Alternative off-road start

A For a more testing alternative from Horton to Old Ing follow the bridleway running steeply uphill immediately behind the Crown Hotel. Just under 5km along this rocky track a footpath (now upgraded to bridleway status) will be found heading **L** (Pennine Way). This leads to Old Ing, where the official route of the PB can be rejoined. This rugged alternative route avoids a 4.8km climb on tarmac.

Looking back towards Pen-y-ghent from Bark House Farm

3 Once through the gate, the track coming in from the right is the Pennine Way footpath (where the alternative off-road route rejoins the official PB).

The PB now heads **L**, due **N**, en route for Ling Gill. Follow the lane, pleasantly downhill, passing the waterfall plunging down the impressive entrance pitch of **Calf Holes**. More easy riding leads around the edge of Fair Bottom Hill, then alongside the picturesque ravine marking the Ling Gill Nature Reserve. **Ling Gill** is crossed via a restored packhorse bridge, after which the trail begins a steady climb towards the summit of **Cam Fell**.

4 Around 120m of painfully 'steady' climbing later, a T-junction of tracks is met at **Cam End** and a welcome rest will be enjoyed at this fabulous viewpoint. The Pennine Way goes off to the **R** here and the PB continues to follow it, climbing again for another steady plod of 3km/120m of even more calf-pumping height gain.

Note In case of emergency a **L** turn at Cam End drops steeply down to the B6255, where another **L** turn will find Ribblehead Station and The Station Inn (bunkhouse). The total distance of this diversion is 4km.

Once past the T-junction the steepness of the Cam High Road begins to show a little mercy. Through a gate, the easy track continues up to a large cairn with signpost, marking the point where the Dales Way branches off right to drop down past the corner of the woodland to Cam Houses Farm.

Wintry conditions on the new bridleway across Swineley Cowm

From this point the views down-valley towards Outershaw, Langstrothdale and Wharfedale are spectacular. This is Dales countryside at its best and well deserves a breather just to admire the view.

A short, steeper section of track leads up to another gate, pretty much marking the end of the main climbing for now. A little further along tarmac is met where a gravel/ tarmac access lane goes off right to Cam Houses Farm. Keep **SA** here. Less than 800m later a short hill marks the approach of another gate.

Immediately through the gate a walled track goes off left, heading almost back in the direction just travelled. However obvious it may appear it is not the right route, being barred by a stone wall after about 100m.

Clinging to life on a Yorkshire gatepost

The correct way is a couple of metres along the road from the walled track, where another gate (also on the **L**) gives access onto open moorland. Initially this path **can be tricky to spot**: by following the line of the walled lane, but keeping about 20m to the right, the correct track will soon be found.

5 This track is also the Ribble Way footpath, firm and grassy with an occasional patch of limestone to negotiate. After about 400m the second of two broken-down walls is crossed. At this point the track bears away from the wall on the left and heads off to the right across open fell.

Note If you have difficulty in locating this vague track, the correct route can be found by simply following the wall on the left around the field edge. After a short distance, the wall turns 90° and heads directly towards Gavel Gap. The official track essentially cuts the corner off the field by heading diagonally across it.

map continues on p80

Although not surfaced, the track is easy to follow and pleasant to ride, until a gate is reached at Gavel Gap. Beyond the gate, a new gravel trail leads on. Easy, downhill riding along the route of the Ribble Way gives those weary leg muscles a well-earned rest.

Watch out at this point for the conspicuous white farmhouse high up on the fellside in the distance ahead. This is Newby Head Farm, and that ominous-looking hill behind and above is where the PB is heading next as it climbs up Wold Fell towards Great Knoutberry Hill.

The splendid downhill journey continues, passing a rather incongruous concrete shed on the way, to eventually end at a farm gate opening out onto the **B6255** at Newby Head Gate, with the road to Upper Dentdale going off more-or-less **SA**.

6 Continue along the Dent road for 400m, where a signposted bridleway on the **R** indicates the beginning of the next climb up the hillside of Newby Head Field (heading roughly due **N**). The climb up to Newby Head Pasture is steep and unrelenting, until a gate finally marks the end of the main climbing. The area around this gate can be muddy, as the trail continues, almost flat now, across a grassy area to yet another gate.

The grassy surface has a track of sorts, which is easy enough to follow. At the end of the valley this trail swings **L**, climbs briefly over the shoulder of the hill, then goes back **R** as it runs close to a wall on the left. Next follows a descent into Swineley Cowm and a short climb up to the head of Arten Gill.

7 Sadly the Pennine Bridleway does not take the easy option of the descent of Arten Gill to the left, nor does it take the pleasant track to the right that heads over to Widdale; predictably it takes the short, steep hill through the metal farm gate **SA**. Mercifully, the climb is short and quickly turns sharp **L** to begin a long traverse around the flanks of **Great Knoutberry Hill**. This ancient drove road is known by a number of names, but 'the Driving Road' seems to be the most used. The excellent track continues around the hill, generally flat or downhill for about 3km, giving easy riding with superlative views across Dentdale and over to Whernside on the other side of the valley.

All too soon tarmac is reached again above the curiously named **Monkeybeck Grains**. In case of emergencies, a left turn here drops steeply

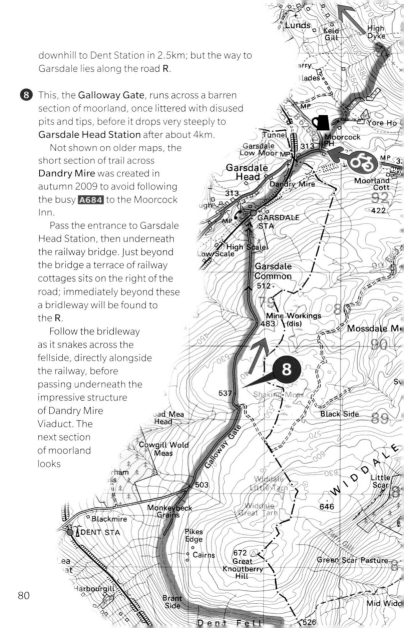

downhill to Dent Station in 2.5km; but the way to Garsdale lies along the road **R**.

8 This, the **Galloway Gate**, runs across a barren section of moorland, once littered with disused pits and tips, before it drops very steeply to **Garsdale Head Station** after about 4km.

Not shown on older maps, the short section of trail across **Dandry Mire** was created in autumn 2009 to avoid following the busy **A684** to the Moorcock Inn.

Pass the entrance to Garsdale Head Station, then underneath the railway bridge. Just beyond the bridge a terrace of railway cottages sits on the right of the road; immediately beyond these a bridleway will be found to the **R**.

Follow the bridleway as it snakes across the fellside, directly alongside the railway, before passing underneath the impressive structure of Dandry Mire Viaduct. The next section of moorland looks ominously boggy, but the skills of the track-layers have been put to expert use, creating a very pleasant riding surface that exits onto tarmac a short distance along the **A684** from the Moorcock Inn.

Cross the road with care, where a continuation of the new bridleway will be found leading directly down to the Moorcock Inn road junction and the end of this section of the ride.

A new section of bridleway leads towards the Moorcock Inn (photo: EA Bowness)

The area around the Moorcock Inn has limited facilities and accommodation. There is B&B in the cottage alongside the pub; the Moorcock also offers B&B and serves excellent meals and snacks, but there are no shops nearby.

If planning a visit to Hawes, a **R** turn at the Moorcock Inn leads excitingly down the **A684** to reach the town in a little over 8km. Be aware however, that those kilometres will be hard won on the return route tomorrow.

'Sorry boys – that's Wild Boar Fell and we're over there next!' (photo: Steve Bramall)

The Yorkshire Dales Part 3
Garsdale Head to Ravenstonedale

START	Moorcock Inn, Garsdale Head **SD 797 927**
FINISH	The Fat Lamb, Ravenstonedale **NY 739 023**
DISTANCE	17km (10½ miles)
OFF ROAD	14.5km (9 miles)
ON ROAD	2.5km (1½ miles)
ASCENT	550m (1800ft)
TIME	3–5hrs
MAP	OS Explorer OL19 Howgill Fells & Upper Eden Valley
OVERALL GRADING	■
PUBS	The Fat Lamb, The King's Head and The Black Swan Hotel, Ravenstonedale; various in Kirkby Stephen
CAFÉS	Lune Springs Garden Centre, Newbiggin-on-Lune (2.4km detour); various in Kirkby Stephen

85% OFF ROAD

This section starts with a climb (don't they all?) before gaining the high point on the ancient track known as 'Lady Anne's Highway', more often shortened to 'the High Way'. The name comes from the story that Lady Anne Clifford regularly used this road on her travels from her estates in Skipton to Pendragon and Appleby. Not very long ago, this green lane was virtually impassable in places but the route has now been closed to motor vehicles and extensively resurfaced to provide a superb riding experience, high above the Mallerstang Valley and the head of the infant River Eden. This memorable part of the Pennine Bridleway should be treated with respect; Garsdale Head is a remote spot and only small hamlets with minimal services will be encountered until Ravenstonedale is reached, or Kirkby Stephen some 19km down-valley.

Directions

1 Facing the Moorcock Inn, the car park will be found to the left of the buildings, alongside the `B6259`. Just beyond the car park a signposted track goes off **R**, across the moorland towards Cobbles Plantation and the driveway to **Yore House Farm**.

Follow this track to meet the farm drive and a bridge across the infant **River Ure**. Once across do not pass through the farm gate ahead, but take the track that bears **L** along the riverbank and heads up towards Cobbles Plantation.

Bridge over the Ure, Garsdale Head

Immediately beyond the trees, another track turns off **R** through a gate and heads steeply uphill, alongside the plantation. At the top of the first section of woodland, the track turns sharp right and crosses a small stream. Immediately before the stream, however, another track, identified by a wooden post (signposted *PB*) bears off **L**, uphill, across the moorland.

The track keeps immediately to the left of the small stream, following its course as it swings gently leftwards, climbing steadily all the while. A line of wooden posts help guide the way as the indistinct track heads for the opposite field boundary some way ahead. As more height is gained, a small clump of trees will draw into view, alongside a significantly larger stream (Johnston Gill). On reaching Johnston Gill turn sharp **R** and climb more steeply towards a wall on the top of the hill. Just to the left of a ruined limekiln, a gate gives access to an obvious track on the other side of the wall.

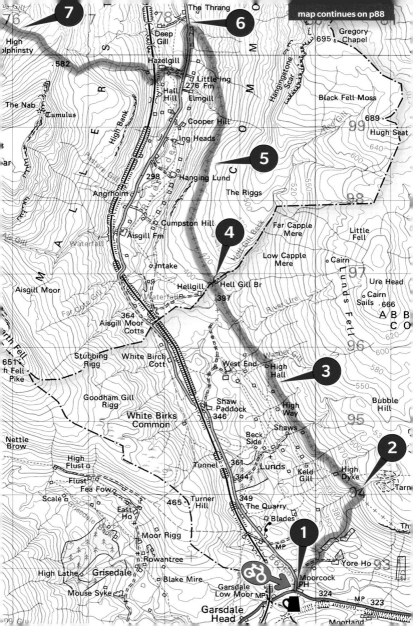

map continues on p88

2 This is Lady Anne's Highway (the **High Way**), which should be followed to the **L**, soon passing the abandoned buildings at **High Dyke**. Once on the High Way both riding and navigation are delightfully easy with the only difficulties being a couple of deep fords, which can become slippery in wet conditions, and a short, flagged stairway, which those of a nervous disposition may choose to walk down.

3 More abandoned buildings are passed just before the ford at **High Hall** and, a little under a mile further along, a prominent farm track will be found climbing up the hillside from the left. This is an alternative bridleway, coming up from Shaw Paddock Farm (a possible escape route to Garsdale Head). Continue towards the distinctive clump of trees marking **Hell Gill Bridge**, just ahead. Take time here to peer carefully over the bridge parapet into the impressive ravine of Hell Gill – as near as one can get to a cave passage with the roof taken off!

4 Pass through the gate at the far side of Hell Gill Bridge and begin the gentle climb up Hellgill Wold. By following the wall on the left navigation is easy until, after about 1.5km, the wall turns away from the track at a truly spectacular viewpoint marked by an equally impressive sculpture.

'Water Cut' by Mary Bourne. The trail up to High Dolphinsty can just be made out between the stones (photo: Steve Bramall)

5 The sculpture ('Water Cut') provides a convenient resting place to admire the views before beginning the wonderful descent immediately ahead, 1km of downhill bliss. A good gravel surface; the occasional ford and drainage ditch to focus the attention; and only the odd suicidal sheep to impede progress. A gate eventually ends the fun as an exit is made onto the `B6259` just south of the large B&B farmhouse at **The Thrang**.

6 To reach the start of the climb up to **High Dolphinsty**, turn **L** (up-valley) along the road for a few hundred metres. Here, a farm track signposted as a bridleway heads off right to **Hazelgill Farm**. Follow the track through the farm gate then, just before the farmhouse is reached, a track goes off **L** towards barns and farm machinery.

Take this track, which quickly turns **R** up alongside the farm buildings, following some small bridleway posts. Once past the buildings the lane is easy to follow uphill to the **L** along the railway embankment. After a short, steep climb, the track passes under the railway, gains a little more height, then hairpins back on itself, climbing steadily all the while.

Just after a ford near a stone barn, the track turns sharp **L** to run by a small stream cascading down the hillside. The track is well surfaced and would give easy riding if only it didn't go up, and up! Eventually a farm gate is reached and, after another steep little pull, the gradient relents a little. A good gravel track is followed until the next steep section arrives, at the top of which the track ends abruptly.

Take care at this point: it is the only place on the route where the correct way ahead is not obvious. To find the continuation of the bridleway head more-or-less **SA**, up a small rise, where a line of bridleway posts will become evident. Follow these posts to soon find a more obvious track heading up to the correct dip in the skyline. As the summit is reached all that effort expended on the climb is rewarded by a wonderful view across the small gate on the right: mile after mile after mile of quality trail – and all of it downhill.

7 Route-finding is not a problem here. There is only one track and it is in excellent condition, giving fantastic riding with minimal effort. A couple of fords give brief respite to the downhill charge until a junction is met just above the buildings of **High Stennerskeugh Farm**. Ignore the track dropping down towards the farm buildings and follow the higher trail as it swings round to the **L**.

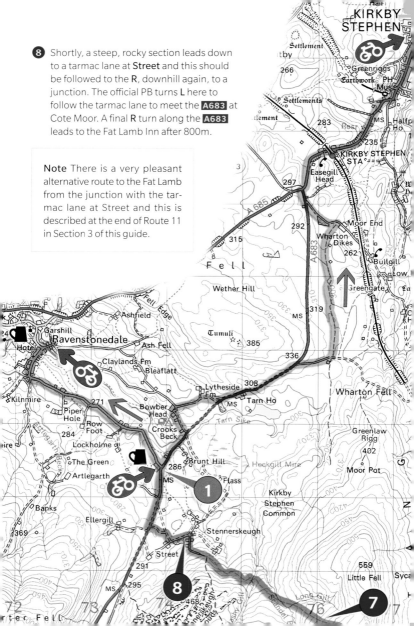

8 Shortly, a steep, rocky section leads down to a tarmac lane at **Street** and this should be followed to the **R**, downhill again, to a junction. The official PB turns **L** here to follow the tarmac lane to meet the **A683** at Cote Moor. A final **R** turn along the **A683** leads to the Fat Lamb Inn after 800m.

Note There is a very pleasant alternative route to the Fat Lamb from the junction with the tarmac lane at Street and this is described at the end of Route 11 in Section 3 of this guide.

And so the official end of the Pennine Bridleway is reached (or, rather, the end until such time as the whole route can be completed). The proposed northern extension (see Introduction) will set off across country from the Fat Lamb, bypassing Ravenstonedale.

The Fat Lamb is a very pleasant pub, situated in an impressive location at the foot of the Howgill Fells; yet somehow ending the ride here feels something of an anti-climax after a journey of over 320km. Essentially, the Fat Lamb is a country inn on a road junction in the middle of the Cumbrian countryside. In view of this you may wish to celebrate the successful completion of your journey in traditional fashion, but then travel a little further to find a more populated location. There are two main contenders for that honour.

1 **Ravenstonedale** is 2.5km along the road that turns **L** by the Fat Lamb Inn. It is a very attractive country village with a couple of pubs and a shop. More extensive services and facilities, however, will be found in Kirkby Stephen, a bustling little town with a railway station.

Passing through the disused workings above High Stennerskeugh; avoid the track leading down to the farm

Alternative finish in Kirkby Stephen

From the Fat Lamb follow the `A683` towards **Kirkby Stephen** (**N**) and take the minor road **L** to Bowber Head, alongside Crooks Beck. Once in **Bowber Head** climb a short rise to a T-junction with a lane coming in from Ravenstonedale. Turn **R** to join up with the `A683` again after a short distance, just before meeting **Tarn House Farm**.

Once past the farm, climb the steep little hill ahead with nice views of the tarn on the right until, on easier ground at the top of the hill, a minor lane goes off **R** (signposted *Mallerstang*). This is Tommy Road (which, if followed to its conclusion, would lead down to Pendragon Castle in the Mallerstang Valley, climbed out of so painfully earlier in the day).

Tommy Road drops downhill, and soon crosses a cattle grid. Immediately over the cattle grid, a signposted bridleway heads off alongside the wall on the **L**. This bridleway (easy and pleasant riding, but a little soft in places after wet weather) runs close by the wall across the moortop to meet a tarmac lane (Bullgill Lane) at **Moor End**.

Turn **L** up the tarmac lane, which quickly meets the `A683` again just south of a junction with the (much busier) `A685`. Turn **R** to meet this junction then **R** (downhill) along the `A685` to find Kirkby Stephen Station, on the **R**, after 800m.

Pass under the railway then immediately turn **R** into the station entrance drive. On the **L** here will be found a new footpath/cycleway that runs alongside the `A685` and, after 800m, climbs a short, steep hill to a minor road. **Kirkby Stephen** town centre will be found by turning **L** here and continuing downhill for a further 1.5km.

Note One major aim of the Pennine Bridleway team has been to avoid the necessity to travel along major roads on this National Trail. Technically, this final extension to Kirkby Stephen station is not part of the main trail but Cumbria County Council and the Pennine Bridleway team are currently seeking a route that will take users to the station while cutting out any use of this busy road. All new developments will be posted on the Pennine Bridleway website so check online periodically for the latest situation.

Descending the Coal Road from Dent Station (Route 9; photo: EA Bowness)

Section 3

Day loops off the Pennine Bridleway

Fine views on the descent to Malham Tarn (photo: Steve Bramall)

1 The Settle Loop

START/FINISH	Tourist Information Centre, Settle Market Square **SD 820 637**
DISTANCE	16km (10 miles)
OFF ROAD	12km (7½ miles)
ON ROAD	4km (2½ miles)
ASCENT	510m (1675ft)
TIME	2hrs 30mins–4hrs
MAP	OS Explorer OL41 Forest of Bowland & Ribblesdale
OVERALL GRADING	■
PUBS	Various in Settle and Giggleswick
CAFÉS	Various in Settle town centre (Ye Old Naked Man Café is particularly bike friendly)
RAILWAY ACCESS	Settle Station on the Settle–Carlisle line. From the station yard, follow signposts for Town Centre. From here the Market Square is easy to locate.

75%
OFF ROAD

The Settle Loop was the first section of the Pennine Bridleway to be opened in the Yorkshire Dales National Park. The route climbs steeply out of Settle, initially on very quiet, virtually traffic-free lanes and later by using a rocky but well-surfaced bridleway, to climb to the high point of the route on Kirkby Fell. From here, the loop turns for home across some superb, upland limestone scenery, with stunning views over Malham Tarn and onto Pen-y-ghent and Ingleborough. The return to Settle is largely downhill and uses a recently resurfaced bridleway that gives excellent riding, with glorious views all around.

Now make no mistake, the first 6.5km of the loop are steadily uphill, climbing about 370m in total, and they are going to hurt a little! Luckily, a substantial portion of this section is on tarmac, which makes the riding a little easier and the views all around amply make up for the effort expended in getting up there. The secret is to take it easy, stop regularly for drinks and enjoy the thought that the downhill return is going to be superb.

The Tourist Information Centre in Settle town centre (Cheapside) is a good starting point. Located in the Market Square, right in the centre of town, it is very easy to find. For those made of sterner stuff, there is an alternative start to the loop that uses off-road lanes to gain the first 150m of ascent. Have fun!

DIRECTIONS

1 With the door of the TIC behind you, turn **L** and go up a short distance to a junction with High Street (not to be confused with the main road through town, called Duke Street). Turn **R** here to quickly meet a T-junction with Victoria Street. A prominent estate agency should be directly ahead, while to the left will

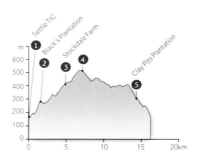

be found a charming example of a 17th-century merchant's house called 'The Folly'. Continue **SA** along the cobbled lane of Victoria Street where, at the next junction, the route climbs to the **L** (signposted *Kirkby Malham and Airton*).

You will now be panting up Albert Hill where, on approaching the top, a Y-junction will be met, complete with PB guidepost (*Long Preston 3½ miles*). The main road goes left, climbing steeply uphill again, but do not take it. Instead, continue on the gentler gradient of the lane to the **R**, which levels out to run along the very quiet Mitchell Lane (signposted *No Through Road*).

Just as the last few buildings are left behind and you dare to hope that you are going to escape the climbing completely, Mitchell Lane begins its own painful ascent. The tarmac surface gives good riding, however, as height is steadily gained and the views down over Settle and Ribblesdale begin to open up behind.

Eventually, after about 1.5km, the gradient eases and the tarmac lane runs out at a junction of tracks alongside **Black's Plantation**. To the right is signposted *Long Preston 2¾ miles*, where the alternative off-road start

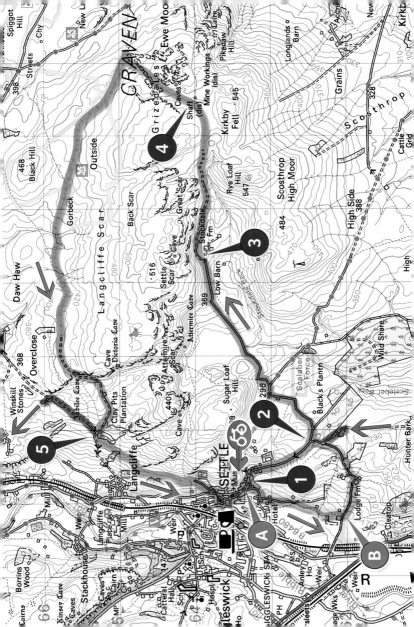

rejoins the main route. However, do not take this lane; the onward route is conveniently signposted *Settle Loop* and it continues more-or-less **SA**.

Note If you are riding the PB as a linear route and have just climbed up from Long Preston past Hunter Bark and Black's Plantation, this is the point where a decision will have to be made as to whether to tackle the Settle Loop or, alternatively, to shoot off down the tarmac lane to the **L** to visit the town.

ALTERNATIVE OFF-ROAD START

. . . .

Ⓐ With the door of the TIC behind you, turn **L** and go up a short distance to a junction with High Street (not to be confused with the main road through town, Duke Street). Turn **R** here to quickly meet a T-junction with Victoria

A 'steady trog' up Stockdale Lane (photo: Steve Bramall)

Street. A prominent estate agency should be directly ahead, while to the left will be found a charming example of a 17th-century merchant's house called 'The Folly'. Continue **SA** along the cobbled lane of Victoria Street until, after a short distance, Commercial Street branches off to the **R**. Leave behind the PB route to speed off, downhill now, on a new adventure. At some point on this short descent, Commercial Street becomes Ingfield Lane, but just continue gently downhill while watching out carefully on the **L** for an obvious, unsurfaced, farm lane (Brockhole Lane).

A glance at the map here will show that Brockhole Lane is a footpath and therefore out of bounds to wheels or hooves. However, in spring 2010 the lane was officially upgraded to bridleway status so cyclists can now take advantage of its considerable charms. Easy riding, including an intriguing section where the track runs side-by-side with a stream for a short distance, leads past Fish Copy barn then on to the farm buildings at Hoyman Laithe.

(B) This is the junction with Lodge Road, where a **L** turn leads to a steep climb beside a small stream up to the impressive buildings of **Lodge Farm**. Just beyond the farm buildings, the bridleway becomes unsurfaced, then turns sharp **L** to cross the beck and begin to climb past a plantation of trees on the **R** (Hudsa Plantation).

The gradient begins to ease as **Black's Plantation** is approached, and another lane soon joins from the right as you reach the trees (this is the PB coming up from Long Preston towards Settle). Continue **SA** at this junction to quickly meet another T-junction at the far end of the plantation. This is the meeting point with the main route description (which joins from the hill on the left).

(2) The riding now becomes off-road, along the pleasant riding surface of Lambert Lane. At this point, the gradient has moderated considerably, although the overall trend remains steadily upwards! On, past Preston's barn, Lambert Lane eventually meets tarmac again at a junction with High Hill Lane. Follow this road to the **R** for only a short distance (100m), where a very quiet road signposted *Stockdale Lane* goes off **L**.

Climb steadily on tarmac here, enjoying wonderful views over the limestone landscape of **Attermire Scar** to the left, complete with the impressive gashes of Attermire and Horseshoe caves. Stockdale Lane undulates pleasantly for 2km, with fine views all around until two gates are met side-by-side. The right-hand gate drops down to Stockdale Farm, but ignore this and take the **LH** gate (signposted *Pennine Bridleway, Malham 3½ miles*).

Traversing high above Settle

3 Route-finding is not a problem here as the rocky track is followed around the flanks of **Great Scar**, with **Rye Loaf Hill** across the valley to the right. The riding surface changes occasionally, from rocky track to pleasant grassy slope and back to rocky track again, through numerous gates, as it climbs steadily to the obvious pass ahead. Although mainly uphill, the track is generally rideable until the summit is approached, where **a couple of short, rocky sections** will test the resolve, stamina and skill of all but the most seasoned of riders.

The top of the pass is finally reached at a small gate, where a stretch of newly repaired gravel track leads off ahead with superb views over towards Malham and Wharfedale. The gravel track gives way to more grassy riding until another gate is reached after a short distance.

The ongoing track passing through the gate is signposted *Cove Road in 1¼ miles* and a detour can be made down it to extend the ride to visit Malham Cove. The Settle Loop, however, does not pass through the gate; instead, it follows the wall to the **L** towards Malham Tarn. The track is not too difficult to locate on the grassy surface, as it keeps close to the wall until, after about 200m, the remains of the ancient Nappa Cross will be seen sitting on top of a large boulder in the wall to the right. At this point, the track begins to bear gently away from the wall, heading for the lovely setting of Malham Tarn a little way ahead.

4 Follow the (now obvious) downhill track across lovely grassy terrain, through two gates then on to a further gate and T-junction of tracks. A prominent signpost here indicates that Langscar Gate is 800m to the right, but the route home is along the track to the **L**, signposted *Langcliffe 4¼ miles* (and what splendid miles they are going to be!).

Initially, the track climbs steadily again on a rutted but rideable grassy surface, until gravel is reached at another gate. Rest here and let your heart rejoice at the view that unfolds before you! Pen-y-ghent and Ingleborough rise majestically ahead, while the track home is downhill as far as the eye can see, on a pristine gravel surface (Gorbeck Road).

After approximately 3km the gravel track changes into a pleasant grassy surface, but soon returns to gravel again. Still further along, the open fell gives way to a walled lane, which descends to a gate and a more traditional farm track. Follow this track, still downhill, to a double gate and cattle grid, after which the track descends a few further metres to a junction with a road, high above the village of **Langcliffe** and alongside **Clay Pits Plantation**.

Note For those riding the PB as a linear route, the Settle Loop rejoins the PB here (see note box on page 64).

---

5 Resist the temptation to tear off down the tarmac here, because the route home takes the signposted bridleway immediately off through the gate on the **L** (signposted *Settle 2 miles*), which is actually the PB climbing out of Settle en route for Stainforth.

Pass through the gate and follow the narrow trail as it traverses pleasantly around the hillside, with more fantastic views down into the valley. A short descent and climb across a dry gully leads to a gate alongside a copse of trees and a further short run to another gate. Once through this gate, a pleasant traverse heads diagonally down the field to an **awkward, rocky step** (which may well require a dismount). Bear sharp **L** after this obstacle and aim for a wall on the **R** to reach yet another gate, which is on an easy-to-follow trail.

A very satisfying, grassy track now leads through a number of further gates and soon enters a walled lane. The way then drops pleasantly downwards, encountering a couple of **entertainingly rocky steps** before meeting a farm gate alongside an old ruined barn.

The continuation of the lane is on an excellent riding surface, with potentially enlivening drainage humps until tarmac is finally reached again at a small group of houses on the outskirts of **Settle**. Follow the bridleway sign downhill into the town, bearing **R** at the next junction, and following the lane down into the Market Square and the end of the ride.

A fine day for a ride

2 Feizor, Wharfe and Catrigg Force

START/FINISH	Buck Haw Brow on the B6480 **SD 796 658**
RETURN VIA FEIZOR	
DISTANCE	12km (8 miles)
OFF ROAD	11.25km (7½ miles)
ON ROAD	0.75km (½ mile)
ASCENT	250m (815ft)
TIME	1hr 30mins–3hrs
OVERALL GRADING	●
ALTERNATIVE RETURN VIA CATRIGG FORCE	
DISTANCE	20.75km (13 miles)
OFF ROAD	11km (6¾ miles)
ON ROAD	9.75km (6 miles)
ASCENT	555m (1825ft)
TIME	2hrs 30mins–4hrs
OVERALL GRADING	■
MAPS	OS Explorers OL2 Yorkshire Dales (Southern & Western areas), OL41 Forest of Bowland & Ribblesdale
PUBS	Various in Settle and Giggleswick; The Craven Heifer, Stainforth
CAFÉS	Various in Settle town centre (Ye Old Naked Man Café is particularly bike friendly); Elaine's Tearooms, Feizor
RAILWAY ACCESS	Settle Station on the Settle–Carlisle line (see below for directions to start)

95%
OFF ROAD

A lovely and highly recommended route giving spectacular views over Ingleborough and Pen-y-ghent with surprisingly gentle climbing. The outward leg of the route, across Giggleswick Scar to Feizor, is retraced on the return journey. However, a very pleasant (but longer and more strenuous) alternative return can be made via the village of Stainforth and the impressive waterfall of Catrigg Force.

This route can be started directly from Settle town centre, but be aware that the first section will pass through the outskirts of Giggleswick, then climb up and up alongside Giggleswick Scar to Scar Top Garage (along the B6480 in the direction of Clapham, Ingleton and Kendal). I prefer to drive up to the top of the scar and park in the convenient lay-by directly opposite the (now disused) garage.

To access the start from **Settle Station**, follow signposts from the station yard to the Market Square. Turn **L** along the **B6480** and follow it through town, across the River Ribble and on towards **Giggleswick**. Do not turn off the main road into Giggleswick village, but follow the **B6480** alongside **Giggleswick Scar** and the local golf club, as the road begins to climb more steeply towards Scar Top Garage on Buck Haw Brow.

The initial climb through Giggleswick Scar

DIRECTIONS

1 Please note that the gate leaving from the lay-by itself is **not** the bridleway. The actual route can be found through a signposted gate, directly opposite the house attached to Scar Top Garage, about 20m back down the hill and neatly hidden in the hedgerow – **so look carefully**. The trail first climbs through a gap in the limestone scar, but although steep the climb is not very long. After 200m a path enters from a gate on the left to cross the bridleway at right angles. It is easy to assume that the bridleway continues straight ahead at this point, but no! Turn **L** through the gate towards Feizor then climb the steep, grassy hill, half-**R**, up an obvious track.

At the next field boundary (and gate) the track can clearly be seen dropping down, to the right of a prominent sheepfold, to the bottom corner of the field. On reaching the corner a partially hidden gate leads through into the next field. Once through the gate follow the very pleasant, grassy track across the next field, aiming for the corner of a wall on the other side. From this corner the track follows a continuation of the wall on the left. Pass through another gate and continue to follow the wall for a short distance, until the track bears off **R** to a prominent signpost. The track onwards is very clear, giving a wonderful, speedy descent downhill to the little cluster of farms and houses that make up the hamlet of **Feizor**.

2 Once onto the tarmac road in the village turn **L** then, almost immediately, **R** along a signposted bridleway between farm buildings (Hale Lane). The track is surfaced at first but becomes rockier as the buildings are left behind. Very pleasant riding follows, along a good track between walls, until a junction is reached at a partially ruined barn

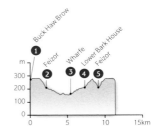

(Meldings Barn). Turn **R** at the barn, along another similar track, to run below **Oxenber Wood** (right). After more excellent riding, a junction of four bridleways is reached.

Note The tracks to the left and straight ahead drop down into Austwick. If looking for food or refreshments, a pub and shop can be found in the village.

The estate agent described it as 'compact and bijou'!

To keep on the route take the track behind you (Wood Lane – a little to the right of the one you have just come down), which climbs a little, turning sharp **L**, then continues to rise more gently before dropping down towards the farm at **Wood End**. Before the farm is reached the track bends sharp **L**, drops down a small hill, then turns back sharp **R** and on into the farmyard. Turn **L** here, down the farm drive to meet a tarmac road on the outskirts of **Wharfe** village.

3 Three bridleways allow alternative routes into the village then back out onto the road. The most pleasant of these can be found by turning **L** down the road for a short distance to Silloth House. Opposite the house will be found an obvious (and pleasant) single-track, which crosses Austwick Beck at Dam House Bridge, then climbs gently into the hamlet. Don't take the first lane out of the village (to the right) but generally aim **SA** (**E**) to find the higher lane back out to the road. On meeting the road, turn **L**, uphill, to climb past White House and Far End farms on the left.

A couple of fields past **Far End Farm** (on the opposite side of the road) is the access drive to **Lower Bark House**. Follow the signposted bridleway up into the farmyard and through a gate (with cattle grid) between the farmhouse and the barns. It is now time to decide which route to take back home!

4 The PB arrives through the gate on your left and continues up the hill to your right, so whichever route is chosen the first section will be along the PB. The shortest route is back via Feizor: turn **R**, behind the barns, and climb steadily up the hill, passing **Higher Bark House**. The track is obvious as it climbs steadily to another gate on the top of the hill, alongside a large, metal sheepfold. Through the gate a very attractive lane climbs a little, then begins to drop down again, gently at first, and then more steeply, back to **Feizor**.

5 Follow the tarmac road through the village, looking out for the bridleway on the **L** that you tore down a little earlier in the day on the outward route. Leaving the PB behind now, climb steadily back up the hill to the signpost. Bear off **R** here to follow the good trail (unfortunately uphill on the way back!) to the junction just above the road at Scar Top Garage. Turn **R** to drop downhill to the road and the end of the ride.

Alternative finish via Catrigg Force

1 From the junction (behind the farmyard) at **Lower Bark House**, turn **L**, passing through another gate into a walled lane. The grassy surface gives easy, downhill riding to another gate at the far end of the lane. This second gate opens out into a field and the track runs straight across, following the line of telegraph poles, to the far side. Approaching the far end of the field a slab bridge is crossed and a further gate gives access to the bottom of another walled lane. This lane immediately turns sharp **L**, and climbs steeply up to the road.

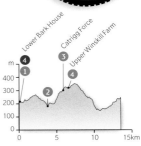

Turn **R** (towards Helwith Bridge); after 400m a crossroads is met, with a minor road going off to the **R** (the left branch leads off towards the quarry complex). The road to the **R** is signposted as being the *PB* and climbs steeply uphill. After the initial steep climb the gradient eases considerably before beginning a pleasant descent into **Little Stainforth**. On entering the village, a road junction is encountered (immediately before the road begins to rise again).

2 Turn **L**, dropping steeply downhill towards the river, alongside a large camping/caravan site. Have fun on the descent, because on the other side of the river bridge an equally steep climb awaits! At the top of the climb the road crosses a bridge over the railway. On the **R** immediately before the bridge however, a new bridleway has been created to cater for travellers on the PB. Follow the walled bridleway as it runs above and alongside the railway, to a junction with a lane. Turn **L** down the lane, which then crosses the railway and leads out to the B6479. Do not follow down as far as the road; just before the busy road is met, a bridleway gate on the **R** allows access into a grassy picnic area.

A track runs down the top edge of this picnic area; follow this as it runs safely under the B6479, via an underpass alongside the beck. **Signposts request riders to dismount as they use the underpass** and mounting blocks are provided at each end of the tunnel for equestrian use. Once on the other side of the main road, the track turns sharp **L** into a car park; the top exit gives access onto one of the main entrances into the village of Stainforth.

Heading back to Settle with Pendle Hill in the far distance

Follow this road to the **R** until a T-junction is met after a few metres. The left branch leads over to Malham, but a **R** turn here leads over Stainforth Beck then on to the Craven Heifer pub.

Opposite the front door of the pub take a **L** turn, further into the village, then another **L** turn, to climb gently up to a junction of lanes in a more open area among cottages. At the top (uphill) corner of this area, a bridleway will be found climbing up the hill towards the popular waterfall of Catrigg Force. The climb is steep (and in places, harshly so!), climbing 90m in less than 800m. Notwithstanding the ascent, the track surface is good and the lane is very attractive, running between drystone walls as it steadily gains height. As the final gradient begins to ease, a copse will be seen in the field to the left. At the higher end of this copse, a gate is met as more open ground is reached.

③ To the left another gate gives footpath access to visit Catrigg Force but, beyond the main gate, a prominent, gravel farm track leads up the hill ahead to another gate on the skyline. **Pay particular attention as this second gate is met**, because once through it, a signposted bridleway will be found, bearing away from the main track to the **R**.

The bridleway is indistinct at first but initially follows the wall on the right-hand side of the field. Essentially, the wall follows the field boundary but the bridleway cuts diagonally across. At the other side of the field, walls on both sides gradually close in to channel the rider into a short section of walled track. The track gives a good riding surface as it follows another wall on the right, along towards the buildings of **Upper Winskill Farm**.

4 Once the gates to Upper and Lower Winskill farms are reached, a PB sign points off up the tarmac lane **L**: the next lung-busting ascent! Although steadily uphill, the climbing is not too severe and the views from here are particularly attractive. Just over 800m later, a junction with a busier road is met at a cattle grid. The climbing is now over for a little while and a well-deserved descent about to start. Turn **R** to cross the cattle grid and begin the descent down the road towards **Langcliffe**. After 800m a small wood comes into view (**Clay Pits Plantation**) and the road takes a sharp turn to the **R**, to drop down much more steeply.

Watch very carefully here! Just as the sharp bend is reached (but before the road begins to steepen) a bridleway will be found heading off through a gate on the **LH** side of the road (signposted *Settle 2 miles*). This single-track bridleway is actually the PB climbing out of Settle en route for Stainforth, and should be followed as it traverses pleasantly around the hillside, with more fantastic views down into the valley.

A short descent and climb, across a dry gully, leads to a gate alongside a copse of trees. There then follows a continuation of the track, alongside the wall, to another gate. Once through this second gate, a further pleasant traverse heads gently downhill, across the field to an awkward, rocky step (which may well require a dismount). Bear sharp **L** after this obstacle, aiming for a gate in the wall ahead.

A very satisfying, grassy track now leads through a number of gates and soon enters a walled lane. The way then drops pleasingly downwards, encountering a couple of entertaining rocky steps before meeting another gate alongside an old ruined barn. The continuation of the lane gives an excellent riding surface, with potentially tricky drainage humps, until tarmac is finally reached again at a small group of houses on the outskirts of **Settle**. Follow the bridleway sign, downhill into the town, bearing **L** at the next junction, and following the lane down into the Market Square to emerge just up from the TIC.

Continue straight through the square to meet the main road through town (**B6480**) at a junction with traffic lights. Turn **R** along the **B6480** and follow it across the River Ribble and on towards Giggleswick. Do not turn off the main road into Giggleswick village, but follow the **B6480** alongside Giggleswick Scar and the local golf club, as the road begins to climb more steeply towards Scar Top Garage and your transport home.

The first steep section of Long Lane

3 Clapham, Crummack Dale and Feizor

START/FINISH	Clapham village, main car park SD 745 692
DISTANCE	18.5km (11½ miles)
OFF ROAD	17km (10½ miles)
ON ROAD	1.5km (1 mile)
ASCENT	465m (1525ft)
TIME	2hrs 30mins–4hrs
OVERALL GRADING	■
MAPS	OS Explorers OL2 Yorkshire Dales (Southern & Western areas), OL41 Forest of Bowland & Ribblesdale
PUBS	The New Inn, Clapham; The Game Cock Inn, Austwick
CAFÉS	Croft Café, Clapham; Elaine's Tearooms, Feizor
RAILWAY ACCESS	Clapham Station on the Skipton–Lancaster line (see below for directions to start). **Note** This is not the Settle–Carlisle line

Clapham is a delightful little village in North Yorkshire, nestled snugly at the base of Ingleborough and roughly midway between Ingleton and Settle. There is a large car park and enough shops and cafés to provide all life's little essentials. This ride gives a perfect blend of rocky trail and grassy fellside with superlative views throughout. A cracking little route and one that is justifiably popular!

To access the start from **Clapham Station**, follow the road signposted *A65 and Clapham village*. After 1.2km, the A65 will be met. Cross this busy road with care and follow the continuation of the lane into **Clapham** centre in 400m. The route begins from the main car park in the centre of the village.

DIRECTIONS

① This is a very entertaining ride almost right from the start. Leave the car park, turning **R** along the quiet road (past the entrance to **Ingleborough Hall**) and towards the church.

Just before the church, an unsurfaced track (Thwaite Lane) goes off **R** and disappears into two short tunnels. This section is understandably **dark, rocky and entertaining** but the surface is rideable and the tunnels mercifully short. The track now climbs steeply on a rocky surface: pushing the bike may be the preferred option here. A steady plod emerges from the woods into a more open area on top of the hill, with fine views all around.

② A junction of tracks will be met alongside **Thwaite Plantation**. The lane going off **L** is the onward route (the lane heading straight towards you is the PB from Austwick, which now turns right to join the Clapham loop). This is Long Lane, which initially drops steeply before beginning a long, steady ascent, high above the popular tourist attractions of Clapdale Drive and **Ingleborough Cave**. Long Lane eventually levels out, and even drops downhill a little, before beginning its final steep, rocky climb to a farm gate, opening out onto grassy fellside. Once through the gate the track can be easily seen, climbing diagonally **R** up the fellside to another gate.

Pass through this gate and continue to the next wall corner, where the track divides and a little confusion may occur: but both tracks soon meet up again on top of the hill. The higher path climbs to a cairn on the skyline ahead, but the **LH** (lower) track gives the easier route as it climbs gently to the left, through **Long Scar**, before swinging back to the **R** towards the summit plateau a little way ahead.

It's very dark in there!
Tunnels on Thwaite Lane
(photo: Geoff Cater)

③ Approaching the top, the main trail continues **SA** at a point where another, well-used track, branches off to the **R**. Take this (narrower) track up to a fine viewpoint looking down over Crummack Dale. As the final crest of the hill is reached, a wide, obvious track is encountered, running at right angles to the path (north–south) along the plateau.

> **Note** At this junction, a clear track drops more-or-less straight ahead down the hill towards Crummack Dale. Although this track is marked on the map (and many riders use it as a convenient descent route) it is not designated as a bridleway or even a footpath.

The official bridleway (and the Clapham route) turns **L** (**N**) at the junction, along a broad, grassy track for 800m to where another junction is met.

4 The PB continues straight ahead towards Sulber Nick and Horton-in-Ribblesdale, our route turns sharp **R** and heads back almost in the same direction you have just come from, climbing very gently, before beginning an exhilarating descent into Crummack Dale. After about 400m of super descent, the track merges with the 'unofficial' track (see box above) coming down the hill from the **R**. Continue downhill, on an easily followed grassy track, to a junction with a fingerpost near a wall.

5 Turn **R** here and follow the wall down to the outskirts of **Crummack Farm**. Two gates, in quick succession, avoid the farmyard and give access to the main farm drive. Follow it, still downhill, across a cattle grid, then further down to where a bridleway sign indicates a junction off to the **L**. Take this onto an unsurfaced farm track and follow it down to a ford (and attractive slab bridge) across Austwick Beck.

The continuation of the lane gives more excellent descent, on narrow single-track between walls. A couple of rocky steps add variety to the downhill run until the track passes a barn on the right. A little way beyond this barn, watch out carefully for a narrow continuation of the bridleway as it follows the wall on the left very closely, up a slight rise, and along to a remarkably tiny cottage.

6 Keep **L**, behind the cottage, then pass directly by the front door of another. Now continue on to meet a track coming up a small hill from the right, which leads **L** again, out to the road. Turn **L** and climb a slight rise, passing the driveway leading to a farm (The White House). Continue a little further along the road, passing the drive to Far End Farm (left).

A short distance further on from here a signposted bridleway on the **R** leads up to the farm at **Lower Bark House**. Follow this lane up into the farmyard, turning **L** just past the end of the main farmhouse, to pass through a gate and over a cattle grid. Once through the gate from the farmyard, turn **R** along the farm track leading gently uphill, behind the barns, towards Higher Bark House and **Wharfe Wood**. (The bridleway joining from the left, behind the farmhouse, has recently been restored and is the route of the PB from Stainforth.)

Once **Higher Bark House** is passed, a gate is encountered, and beyond this the track remains easy to follow as it climbs steadily to another gate (and large metal sheepfold) approaching the top of the hill. Through this gate, a short climb leads to the summit, where a very attractive lane drops down, gently at first, and then more steeply, into the hamlet of **Feizor**.

7 A gate leads onto the tarmac road running through the village (Feizor has no shops but there is a pleasant café in the centre). Follow this road until it crosses a cobbled ford (which is often dry) then, just on the next bend, turn **R** along a signposted bridleway between farm buildings (Hale Lane). The track is surfaced at first but becomes rockier as the buildings are left behind. Excellent riding now follows, along a good track between walls, until a T-junction is reached at a partially ruined barn (Meldings Barn) where a continuation of the track crosses a small ford then runs below **Oxenber Wood** (right).

More fantastic riding leads, after about 800m, to a junction of four bridleways. Keep **SA**, downhill, to a substantial ford across Austwick Beck, with a convenient slab bridge to the left (Flascoe Bridge). Once across the beck follow the continuation of the lane out to meet the Austwick-to-Wharfe road on the outskirts of **Austwick** (turn left to visit the village). Turn **R** along the road towards Wharfe. Around 400m later, a signposted bridleway will be found on the **L** and this should be followed to where the rocky track turns sharp **L** as it passes Slaindale Barn. The continuation of the bridleway now begins to climb steeply until, approaching the top of the hill, a junction with a quiet road (Crummack Lane) is met.

8 Straight over at the junction, the obvious track of Thwaite Lane will be found, which, following extensive regrading, gives an excellent riding surface as it climbs steadily up to Long Tram Plantation (left). The riding becomes easier now with fine views over to Norber and Crummack Dale to the right.

After about 1.5km of further pleasant riding, a large plantation is met as Thwaite Lane prepares for its rocky descent into **Clapham** (the lane off to the right here is Long Lane, on the outward route). Keep **SA** at the junction and follow the rocky track down into the village passing through the disconcertingly dark tunnels on the way. A **L** turn along the road leads into the village and the end of an excellent outing.

*Delightful riding over a spring meadow
on the approach to Wharfe*

4 Horton-in-Ribblesdale, Helwith Bridge and Sulber Nick

START/FINISH	Horton-in-Ribblesdale, main car park **SD 788 746**
DISTANCE	20km (12½ miles)
OFF ROAD	10.75km (6¾ miles)
ON ROAD	9.25km (5¾ miles)
ASCENT	430m (1410ft)
TIME	2hrs 30mins–4hrs
OVERALL GRADING	●
MAP	OS Explorer OL2 Yorkshire Dales (Southern & Western areas)
PUBS	The Crown Hotel and The Golden Lion Hotel, Horton; the Helwith Bridge, Helwith Bridge
CAFÉS	The Pen-y-ghent Café, Horton
RAILWAY ACCESS	Horton-in-Ribblesdale Station on the Settle–Carlisle line (see below for directions to start)

55% OFF ROAD

Half of this ride is on tarmac, while the other half is on pleasant tracks and grassy trails. In addition there is only one major climb, leading to spectacular views in a dramatic setting. These two factors combine to make this trip an ideal datum point for rides within this book. Tick the Horton route off and you will be confident in your ability to tackle the next green route, or to move up to attempt a blue.

The village of Horton-in-Ribblesdale is the ideal starting point in that it has all the usual tourist facilities and the railway station is perfectly situated for those wishing to use this mode of transport. The route description begins from the pay-and-display car park (complete with toilets) in the centre of the village.

To access the start from the station at **Horton-in-Ribblesdale**, follow the exit signs out onto the `B6479`. Continue **SA** at the junction, which leads to a bridge across the River Ribble directly alongside the Crown Hotel. The road immediately swings sharp **R** to cross another bridge and, a short way further along, the car park will be found on the right of the road.

DIRECTIONS

1 Leave the car park by turning **R** along the `B6479` towards Helwith Bridge and Settle. Continue through the village, passing an excellent 'outdoor friendly' café on the right and the village shop a little

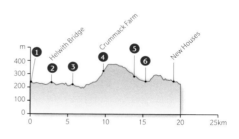

further along on the left. Just past the church, the `B6479` turns sharp **L** then crosses a stream again at Horton Bridge. Easy riding follows the road for a further 2.75km passing farms at Dry Beck and **Studfold**, until a junction is met at **Helwith Bridge**.

2 At this junction, the `B6479` turns sharp left as it continues towards Stainforth and Settle but turn **R** onto the minor road leading to Wharfe and Austwick. Almost immediately, the road crosses the **River Ribble** again, passing alongside the Helwith Bridge pub with the untidy infrastructure of a large quarry on the right. (After 800m a minor road drops down a small hill on the left to join the route; a signpost indicates that this is the PB from Stainforth, which joins the Horton loop for a little while). Keep **SA** at the junction, heading towards Wharfe and Austwick.

About 400m further along, watch out for a PB fingerpost, indicating a junction on the **L**, into a walled lane. The grassy track drops down a short hill and through a gate into open fields. Once through the gate, the track crosses a slab bridge and then runs across the middle of the field, generally following the path of a line of prominent telegraph poles. At the far end of the field, the track enters a walled lane, with a grassy riding surface, before climbing up to **Lower Bark House**.

How are your calves?

3 Through a gate, a junction is met, with the PB taking the left-hand option, up
towards Higher Bark House. Our route however, takes the **RH** track, which
passes through another gate into the main farmyard area, then follows the
farm drive out to meet tarmac again. At the end of the farm drive from Lower
Bark House, turn **L** down the road for about 800m, passing entrances to
Far End and White House farms on the way.

   Where the road turns sharp left and begins to drop downhill, a
bridleway is signposted going off **SA** into **Wharfe**. Follow the unsurfaced
track into the hamlet, keeping **R** where it splits at another bridleway
signpost. The bridleway runs right across the lawn in front of an attractive
cottage then goes behind what must be one of the smallest cottages in
Yorkshire!

   Another bridleway is then met at a Y-junction just beyond a small, slab
bridge, where the correct route is the branch going off to the **R** (uphill). The
way on now becomes clear, climbing steadily alongside the wall, on a track
that is generally good but has **one or two rocky sections** that will test riding
(or pushing) skills. The climb is steadily uphill, but not excessively steep and
eventually gives way to a pleasant downhill section leading to a ford.

   Be warned that **the ford is deep and rocky**; it makes sense to take the
bridge and guarantee dry feet at the other side. Pleasant riding for a further

few hundred metres meets Crummack Lane coming in from the left. Turn **R** at this junction to climb up the hill towards **Crummack Farm**.

④ Keep to the left of the farm, passing through two signposted gates, and follow the wall on the right up an obvious, wide track, aiming for the gate on the skyline ahead. A little before the gate, a prominent fingerpost points up the hill to the **L**. This is (currently) signposted *Sulber 1¼ miles*. Initially the track is quite easy to follow, as it bears to the left, climbing steeply away from the wall. After the initial steep section, the track levels out a little before splitting at a vague Y-junction.

The track bearing off left then contouring back rightwards seems to give the easier line and is often followed to the top of the hill at Long Scar. Technically, however, this track is not a right of way (although many people use it on a regular basis). The official bridleway is the track going more-or-less **SA** at the indistinct junction, steeply at first, before swinging **R**, to head **N** and then **NE** to reach the top of the hill at an obvious junction of tracks.

Note Unhelpfully the first – unofficial – track also meets the top of the hill at a prominent junction, and it is fairly easy to become a little disorientated at this point! The more southerly junction (the summit of the unofficial track) is easily distinguished by looking over to the left to see a small hill, with a large cairn on top of it.

At the official junction there is no hill to the left, and the left-hand branch of the track just met will be heading off back, almost in the same direction you have just come from. Turn **R** (**N**) to run along the top of the hill, on a well-defined, grassy track with an occasional section of limestone providing a rocky alternative surface (rejoining the PB again after its climb up from Clapham village).

The next section of track gives easy riding to **Sulber** Gate, where a crossing of footpaths – **a popular route for walkers** heading up (and down) Ingleborough – will be found in a spectacular setting above Moughton Scars and Sulber Nick (over the wall right). The bridleway continues **SA** again, across more pleasant terrain, to a gate displaying a sign marking the entrance to Ingleborough Nature Reserve. More excellent riding follows with occasional farm tracks going off at various points. The main trail is never difficult to follow here but, in case of indecision, keep the wall to the left vaguely in sight as you head northwards towards the farm buildings at **Borrins**.

Once through the gate at the other end of the nature reserve, the track turns sharp **R** to detour around the farm, before joining the main farm drive as it drops downhill towards the road. Once around the next **RH** bend, the track straight ahead is the access lane to South House Farm, but a **L** turn here drops downhill again to meet the `B6479`, with great views across upper Ribblesdale.

In case of difficulties at this point, the route can be shortened by turning **R** at this junction and following the `B6479` down into Horton. Mainly downhill, the road bends **L** then back **R** to pass under a railway bridge and enter the outskirts of the village.

5 Continue along the much nicer, official route by crossing the `B6479` and immediately turning **L** (towards Selside) utilising a new path alongside the road. After a few metres a bridleway gate gives access onto a new track

Moughton Scars with Pen-y-ghent in the background (photo: Steve Bramall)

The new bridleway down to the Ribble crossing near Selside (photo: Steve Bramall)

running down the hill to the **R**. This bridleway (not shown on current maps) passes through two farm gates then winds round to the **R** to a tunnel under the railway. Once on the other side of the track, the trail continues to drop down across **Far Moor** to an impressive, newly built, equine-friendly bridge over the **River Ribble**.

6 The bridleway then turns **L**, alongside the river, to meet an access track at **Dale Mire Barn**. This farm track is then followed steeply uphill to the **R** where it meets a very quiet tarmac road, leading from Horton up to farms at High Birkwith. Turn **R** here and follow the tarmac lane down into the village via **New Houses**. The first building met in **Horton** will be the Crown Hotel. Continue past the side of the pub to meet the **B6479** at a junction located directly between two bridges. To return to the start continue **SA** at the junction, crossing the bridge to find the car park a short distance further along on the **R**.

Winter conditions don't stop these boys from getting out!

5 Ribblehead to Ling Gill and Horton-in-Ribblesdale

START/FINISH	Junction of the B6255 and B6479 at Ribblehead Viaduct **SD 765 792**
RETURN VIA SELSIDE	
DISTANCE	25.75km (16 miles)
OFF ROAD	14.5km (9 miles)
ON ROAD	11.25km (7 miles)
ASCENT	564m (1850ft)
ALTERNATIVE RETURN VIA HIGH BIRKWITH	
DISTANCE	27km (16¾ miles)
OFF ROAD	18.25km (11¼ miles)
ON ROAD	8.75km (5½ miles)
ASCENT	657m (2156ft)
TIME	3hrs 30mins–5hrs (both options)
OVERALL GRADING	▲
MAP	OS Explorer OL2 Yorkshire Dales (Southern & Western areas)
PUBS	The Station Inn, Ribblehead; the Crown Hotel, Horton
CAFÉS	The Pen-y-ghent Café, Horton
RAILWAY ACCESS	Ribblehead Station on the Settle–Carlisle line (see below for directions to start)

The Ribblehead Viaduct, a magnificent example of Victorian engineering, stands proudly over the moorland fell of Batty Green, representing years of toil by countless navvies in this wild, uncompromising landscape. The viaduct forms a spectacular, if somewhat sombre, backdrop to the starting point of this memorable ride over the wild moorland of Cam Fell following bridleways and Roman roads.

The exit from **Ribblehead Station** joins the `B6255` alongside a railway bridge and almost directly opposite the Station Inn. Turn **R** along the `B6255` for only a few metres to meet a cattle grid (see paragraph ❶ of the following route description).

To find the starting point from Ingleton take the `B6255` (Ingleton-to-Hawes) road and follow it for 9.5km, passing White Scar Cave and the Old Hill Inn on the way, until the unmistakable outline of the Ribblehead Viaduct looms spectacularly into view. The road passes under the Settle–Carlisle railway by the Station Inn then crosses a cattle grid before dropping down a short hill to where the `B6479` goes off right to Horton-in-Ribblesdale. Immediately beyond this junction, a large lay-by on the right (often with a refreshments caravan) provides ample parking, with plenty of other possibilities in the immediate vicinity.

Directions

❶ Initially, the ride begins gently enough by heading off along the `B6255` towards Hawes (away from Ingleton). After 1.5km **Far Gearstones** outdoor centre is passed on the right and, less than 800m further along, an obvious track leads off to the **R**, through a farm gate and down to a footbridge and ford across **Gayle Beck**.

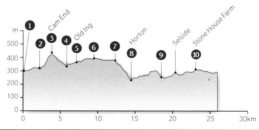

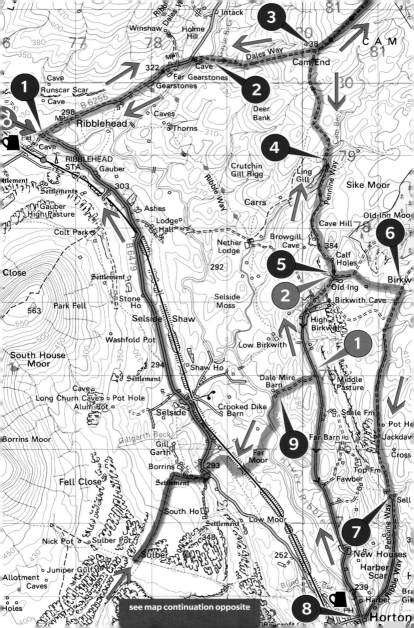

see map continuation opposite

2 This ancient Roman road also carries the Pennine Way and Dales Way long-distance footpaths. Many older maps may still show this well-surfaced track as a footpath, but it is now classed as bridleway and open to cyclists and horse riders. Once over the beck, the way onwards looks ominously upwards and this is indeed the main climb of the day! After 1.5km (and a breathless 120m of ascent) a junction of tracks is reached, approaching the top of **Cam End**.

3 Pause awhile to enjoy superb views of the Three Peaks – Ingleborough, Whernside and Pen-y-ghent – magnificently profiled in all their glory. (The continuation of the track straight ahead will eventually lead, via the Cam High Road, into Hawes or Bainbridge.) Take the track off to the **R**, which drops invitingly downhill on an excellent riding surface, to meet **Ling Gill** beck at a lovely spot complete with packhorse bridge.

4 Once over the bridge, the track runs alongside the impressive gorge of the Ling Gill Nature Reserve as it climbs steadily out of the valley again. The next 1.5km gives lovely riding, along an excellent track, past a barn on the right, which marks a ladder stile and path down to **Browgill Cave**. A little further along, but on the left, another ladder stile gives access to the impressive entrance to **Calf Holes**.

Here the stream plunges spectacularly into blackness only to reappear a little while later at the exit of Browgill Cave, where it continues on its journey as Brow Gill Beck. Take care when looking closely at the entrance to Calf Holes: although an easy beginner's pothole, the rocks can be treacherously slippery.

Continue pleasantly along the lane to meet a junction of tracks next to the farm at **Old Ing**.

5 This is a popular parking area for cavers visiting the numerous caves in the vicinity, so watch out for people clad in all manner of unusual gear preparing to disappear underground! At this point a short cut can be taken (missing out Horton) by taking the track heading off downhill, through the gate to the **R**. This leads down to tarmac at **High Birkwith Farm**, picking up the main route again above **Dale Mire Barn**. The more exciting option, however, takes in Horton. The bridleway providing that descent lies about 800m to the east,

'Nah – I think I'll stick to biking' – the view down Calf Holes

and although the map clearly indicates that the Pennine Way track leading to it is **not** a bridleway, since autumn 2011 Yorkshire Dales National Park Authority have redesignated this particular section.

So, on arriving at Old Ing, take the **LH** farm gate to access the new bridleway. The first section of trail is a wide, well-graded, forestry access road, heading towards a large plantation. After about 200m, the new section of bridleway bears off to the **R** alongside a wall, climbing briefly over the small hill just ahead. About 800m from Old Ing a short descent leads to a T-junction with another rocky bridleway, where you turn **R**.

6 The bridleway heads off across Low Birkwith Moor towards Horton-in-Ribblesdale. It is very easy to follow, on a track that gives a good, if sometimes rocky, riding surface. After a few kilometres of pleasant riding with wonderful views, the trail drops down a short hill to an open area with a stream on the left and a dry, grassy gully on the right.

7 These are the twin entrances of Sell Gill Holes; the stream disappears down the aptly named 'wet route' while the long-abandoned gully provides a dry, alternative entrance, into the extensive cave system beneath. The continuation of the route down into **Horton** will provide its own challenging

Cam High Road with Ribblehead Viaduct in shadow, just above the farm

descent as it drops more steeply now, with some **particularly bouldery sections** to test riding skills, and a final exit onto tarmac in the car park of the Crown Hotel.

Note A left turn along the road here leads to all facilities in the village, including café, shop, pubs and campsite.

8 Don't cross either of the two road bridges from the Crown car park, but instead turn **R** to take the minor road running immediately alongside the pub (leading to High Birkwith Farm and Old Ing). The lane initially follows the river then begins to climb steadily, passing through the hamlet of **New Houses**. Climb more steeply away from the hamlet with views of a tarn and the infant River Ribble down to the left. A little way past the tarn a cattle grid is crossed and, a very short distance beyond this, a bridleway goes off to the **L**, dropping down to **Dale Mire Barn** (a new section of the PB, not shown on older OS maps).

ALTERNATIVE FINISH VIA HIGH BIRKWITH FARM
. . . .

1 For more steep climbing (but also a wonderfully speedy descent), at the junction with the new bridleway above **Dale Mire Barn** continue up the road (also the route that the PB takes over to Garsdale Head). Climb steadily up the road to **High Birkwith Farm** in about 1km to where the tarmac surface ends at a gate alongside the farmyard. Pass through the gate and climb the rocky hill ahead, passing (and ignoring) a junction with a farm track off to the right. A little further up the hill, the farm at **Old Ing** will be found on the right of the track, and another gate is met.

2 Once through the gate, the track on the **L** is the one you rode along earlier in the ride. Follow it now in the opposite direction, to pass **Calf Holes** on the **R** and enjoy a pleasant downhill run to **Ling Gill** bridge. Next comes a long, painful climb back up to the **Cam End** junction, where a **L** turn provides an exhilarating descent back to the **Gayle Beck** ford. It is a short climb back up to the `B6255`, where a **L** turn takes you back to the starting point in just over 2km.

9 On reaching **Dale Mire Barn**, the bridleway turns sharp **L** and runs alongside the river to a new equine-friendly bridge, before climbing back up under the railway to meet the `B6479` just outside the hamlet of Selside. (On reaching the road the PB will be found coming over from Clapham a little to the left.) Turn **R**, along the road, into **Selside**. On leaving the hamlet a lane, usually crowded with cavers visiting the Alum Pot system, is passed on the left as the road swings to the **R** to begin a long, steady climb along Selside Shaw Old Lane. Eventually, the lone farmhouse of **Stone House** marks the end of this section, and also the end of the climbing for today.

10 The road soon turns **R**, across the railway, then swings back **L** along the Gauber road, to arrive at the **Ribblehead** junction with the `B6255`, and the end of the ride, after little more than 1.5km of further riding.

Steep, rocky and exciting!

6 Ribblehead to Dentdale via the Craven Way

START/FINISH	Junction of the B6255 and B6479 at Ribblehead Viaduct **SD 765 792**
DISTANCE	25.75km (16 miles)
OFF ROAD	13.5km (8½ miles)
ON ROAD	12.25km (7½ miles)
ASCENT	655m (2155ft)
TIME	4–6hrs
OVERALL GRADING	▲
MAP	OS Explorer OL2 Yorkshire Dales (Southern & Western areas)
PUBS	The Station Inn, Ribblehead; The Sportsman's Inn, Cowgill
CAFÉS	None on main route; Bernie's Café and Inglesport in Ingleton, or detour 2km to Dent for pubs, shop and café
RAILWAY ACCESS	Ribblehead Station on the Settle–Carlisle line (see below for directions to start)

55% OFF ROAD

The Craven Way is an ancient drove road that traverses the flanks of Whernside en route from Ribblehead to Dentdale. Guarded by a steep ascent from Ribblehead and a rocky, technical descent into Deepdale, the track between the two gives lovely riding in a superb situation. A route not to be missed – once stamina levels and riding skills have been built up!

To access the route from **Ribblehead Station**: from the exit join the **B6255** alongside a railway bridge and almost directly opposite the Station Inn. Turn **R** along the **B6255** for only a few metres to meet a cattle grid (see paragraph **1** of the following route description).

To find the starting point from Ingleton take the **B6255** (Ingleton-to-Hawes) road and follow it for 9.5km, passing White Scar Cave and the Old Hill Inn on the way, until the unmistakable outline of the Ribblehead Viaduct looms spectacularly into view. The road passes under the Settle–Carlisle railway by the Station Inn then crosses a cattle grid before dropping down a short hill to where the **B6479** goes off right to Horton-in-Ribblesdale. Immediately beyond this junction, a large lay-by on the right (often with a refreshments caravan) provides ample parking, with plenty of other possibilities in the immediate vicinity.

Directions

1 To begin the ride, head
towards the Station Inn where, just before the cattle grid is met, a prominent gravel track heads off towards the **Ribblehead Viaduct**. Follow this track (which gives very easy riding) under the viaduct, then continue through a farm gate and along to the farm at **Gunnerfleet**. Pass alongside a group of

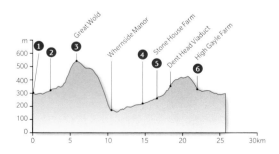

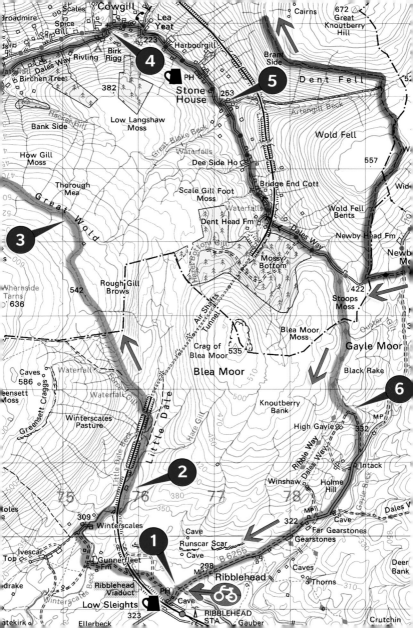

The bridleway running beneath Ribblehead Viaduct (photo: EA Bowness)

barns and outbuildings before crossing the (often dry) **Winterscales Beck** via a small bridge. A **R** turn at the junction here leads up a pleasant, tarmac lane, through another gate, to a T-junction. A further **R** turn leads across a cattle grid before dropping down past **Winterscales Farm** and back across the beck to a gate.

The lane now becomes unsurfaced and rocky as it climbs gently back up towards the railway embankment. Pass through a ford, then a gate, and back under the railway to meet another junction of tracks. To the right the track is signposted as a footpath, but the **L** branch is the bridleway heading up towards Whernside. Take this **LH** option, passing by the signal box and cottage at Bleamoor sidings, on a well-surfaced track giving easy riding.

2 Less than 800m further along, a deep, rocky ford is met, with a convenient bridge allowing an alternative crossing.

> **Note** Also in this area is a prominent track heading off to the right towards some spoil heaps on the hillside ahead. This is the footpath linking the various ventilation shafts servicing the Bleamoor Tunnel, so take particular care not to go shooting off uphill here!

On the other side of the ford, the track continues to a very interesting bridge across the Settle–Carlisle railway, carrying not only the bridleway, but also a sizeable stream. A peer over the right-hand parapet gives good views of the entrance to the Bleamoor Tunnel, before the track continues, through more gates, and begins its climb up Smithy Hill. Much trail renovation has been carried out in this area and this section is paved in a **series of rocky steps that make riding almost impossible.** Take the opportunity for a quick push as the track climbs past the waterfall of **Force Gill**, impressive after rainfall.

Beyond Force Gill a more rideable surface leads up towards Slack Hill and Grain Head. This is the steepest part of the climb: pushing may be the best option. The main climbing ends at a stile on the left where the signposted footpath up Whernside leads off towards Grain Head. However, the bridleway continues **SA** at this point where further trail improvements have provided a rocky but rideable surface. Eventually, another gate marks the end of the main ascent, and a pleasant, grassy surface begins the lovely traverse around Craven Wold.

The next section of trail gives wonderful riding in a superb situation. Over to the right the line of spoil heaps from the construction of the Bleamoor Tunnel can be traced across the moor, while to the left the imposing flanks of Whernside give some shelter from the prevailing weather. Easy riding along the Craven Way gives no route-finding problems as the grassy trail is followed, past a ruined barn and across **Great Wold**.

3 Occasional patches of rutted or boggy trail hint to the previous damage left by motorised vehicles, but most of the track has now recovered to the point where these patches give only minor inconvenience to progress. At 'Boot of the Wold', a farm gate and sheepfold mark where the trail enters a walled section and **the riding becomes more technical.** Although increasingly rocky, the track is still rideable throughout as it begins its long descent towards Dentdale. Numerous gates give opportunities to rest aching wrists and braking fingers while the trail becomes steeper and rockier as the slopes of **Deepdale** are traversed. This is **a fine, technical descent that will fully test riding skills – and brakes!**

Eventually, a telecommunications mast and hut are met and the trail becomes much easier to ride, as a gravel surface continues down towards Dyke Hall Lane. Gravel gives way to concrete (**careful here – the corner is slippery!**) before another gate gives access to a walled farm lane with a grassy riding surface leading out to tarmac at the lower end of Deepdale.

A **R** turn here quickly leads down to a junction with the **Dentdale** road, where another **R** turn continues past the impressively proportioned country house of **Whernside Manor** (once the National Cave Training Centre but now a private residence). Enjoy the next 3km as the quiet road undulates pleasantly along the dale, passing farms and cottages, to reach Ewegales Bridge (and campsite) on the outskirts of **Cowgill**.

4 Glancing ahead, a **very** steep road can be seen climbing up the hillside on the other side of the valley, fortunately not on the route of the loop (it leads to Dent Station); but all roads out of Dent Head are decidedly upwards in nature so rest assured there is an equally steep climb ahead! Once over Ewegales Bridge, turn **R** and continue up-valley. The lane alongside the church is the point where the bridleway from Garsdale comes out (Route 9); ignore this for today and continue along the main valley road, up towards the next bridge at Lea Yeat.

Arriving at **Lea Yeat**, pass the junction with the road heading off left up to Dent Station and Garsdale Head, then turn **R** over the bridge and follow the main road back **L** (up-valley) in a lovely setting alongside the **River Dee**. Soon after, The Sportsman's Inn will be passed and, 500m further along, the road swings **L** to cross the river again at **Stone House Farm** (the road leading straight ahead here is the beginning of the steep climb up Arten Gill, Routes 8 and 9).

5 Turn **R** after the bridge to begin a steep climb up the main road towards **Dent Head Viaduct**. The steepest part is the section up to the viaduct, but once beyond this point, the road continues to climb steadily for another 800m. Eventually the top of the climb is reached approaching **Stoops Moss**. As the gradient begins to ease, watch out carefully on the **R** for a farm gate and bridleway fingerpost.

This is the **Black Rake** road, which gives a convenient route back towards Ribblehead. The single-track bridleway climbs steadily, but relatively gently, to a high point below **Blea Moor Moss**. It then turns a little to the **L** and begins its descent towards **High Gayle Farm**. Just above the farm a junction is met, where a very mossy signpost indicates the Dales Way footpath going off right. Ignore this and follow the obvious track, further downhill, to meet another junction, where the most prominent track turns sharp right towards the farm.

6 The correct route is **SA**, dropping a little further down the hill, passing through a rickety gate and following the wall on the right. After a few

Descending towards Ribblehead on the Black Rake Road

metres of descent, the track swings back sharp **R** to run along (**an often muddy**) farm track and out onto the main drive to High Gayle Farm, just on the downhill side of the gate. Turn **L** down the farm drive to meet the B6255, where a **RH** turn leads back to **Ribblehead** after about 3km of easy road riding.

Cyclists on the B6255 approaching Newby Head Gate (photo: EA Bowness)

7 Cam High Road and the Ribble Way

START/FINISH	Gayle Beck Lodge on the B6255 near Newby Head Gate **SD 791 814**
DISTANCE	15km (9¼ miles)
OFF ROAD	12.5km (7¾ miles)
ON ROAD	2.5km (1½ miles)
ASCENT	335m (1100ft)
TIME	2–4hrs
OVERALL GRADING	◼
MAP	OS Explorer OL2 Yorkshire Dales (Southern & Western areas)
PUBS	None on main route; the Station Inn, Ribblehead
CAFÉS	None on main route; detour to Horton, Ingleton or Dent
RAILWAY ACCESS	Ribblehead Station on the Settle–Carlisle line (see below for directions to start)

85%
OFF ROAD

This relatively short loop circumnavigates Gayle Moor with only moderate climbing. It nevertheless deserves inclusion in this guide because much of the bridleway section is newly created and the trail surface is so good that it can be ridden with the type of mountain bike that may struggle on some of the rockier trails. The route makes a perfect beginner's circuit, providing due regard is made to weather conditions that, at this altitude, can quickly change a lovely day out into a very unpleasant experience indeed! The return route along the Black Rake Road is a little rockier than the graded tracks across Gayle Moor, but a smoother and more direct return to the start point can be made along the B6255 by turning left at Newby Head Gate.

To access this route from **Ribblehead Station** turn **R** to follow the road under the railway, and follow the `B6255` in the direction of Hawes. After 1km the farm at **Far Gearstones** will be seen on the right of the road, and, just after it, an obvious track leads off to the **R**, through a farm gate and steeply downhill to Gayle Beck. Continue from point **2** below.

The route can be joined from the parking areas around Ribblehead Viaduct, but the start point at Gayle Beck Lodge will be found a little further along the road towards Hawes.

To find Ribblehead, take the `B6255` (Ingleton-to-Hawes) road and follow it for 9.5km, passing White Scar Cave and the Old Hill Inn on the way, until the unmistakable outline of the Ribblehead Viaduct draws spectacularly into view.

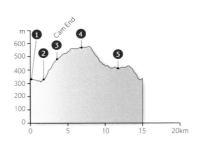

If travelling by train, you will exit from Ribblehead Station at this point.

The road passes underneath the Settle–Carlisle railway alongside the Station Inn, then crosses a cattle grid before dropping down a short hill to where the `B6479` goes off right to Horton-in-Ribblesdale. This junction is the parking area at Ribblehead. To reach the route start point, continue along the Hawes road for a further 3km. A little way beyond the drive to **High Gayle Farm** (left) a ruined cottage (Gayle Beck Lodge) will be found on the right-hand side of the road and convenient parking is located immediately alongside.

DIRECTIONS

1 The ride begins gently enough by heading back along the `B6255` towards Ribblehead. After 1.2km the farm at **Far Gearstones** will be seen on the left of the road, and just before it, an obvious track leads off to the **L**, through a farm gate and steeply down to a footbridge and ford across **Gayle Beck**.

② This ancient Roman road also carries the Dales Way and, a little further up the hill, the Pennine Way, long-distance footpaths. Many older maps may still show this well-surfaced track as a footpath but it is now classed as bridleway and therefore open to bikes and horses. Once over the ford a **particularly steep, cobbled exit slope** will test riding skill before the beginning of the main climb starts to take its toll on stamina reserves. After 1.5km (and a breathless 120m of ascent) a junction of tracks is reached, approaching the top of **Cam End**.

③ The trail joins the PB at this point and goes **SA** at the junction, climbing still further, along the Cam High Road. Soon the steepness relents a little. On the right can be seen an extensive swathe of woodland (**Cam Woodlands**), and one section of the forest crosses the valley then climbs up the hill towards Cam High Road. Once through a gate, the easy track continues up to a large cairn with signpost, marking the point where the Dales Way branches off right to drop down to Cam Houses Farm.

From here the views down-valley towards Outershaw, Langstrothdale and Wharfedale are spectacular. This is Dales countryside at its best and well deserves a quick breather to admire the view.

A short, steeper section of track leads up to another gate and this pretty much marks the end of the main climb. A little further along, tarmac is met where a gravel/tarmac lane goes off to the right down to Cam Houses Farm. Keep **SA** here, in a lovely situation. A tarmac lane – no traffic – virtually flat – and views to die for! What more could you wish for? Less than 800m later a short hill marks the approach of another gate (Cold Keld Gate) and a change in direction.

④ Immediately through the road gate, an obvious walled track goes off left, heading almost back in the same direction just travelled. Ignore this, however, and continue one or two metres further on, where another gate on the **L** gives access onto open fellside. Once through the gate, turn **L** to pick up a vague track, which follows the wall (left).

The track is firm and grassy with an occasional patch of limestone to negotiate. It runs parallel to the wall but a few metres to the right of it. After about 400m the second of two old, broken-down walls is crossed and the track bears away from the wall on the left and heads off, to the right, across open fell.

> **Note** If you have difficulty in locating this vague track, the correct route can be found by simply following the wall on the left around the field edge. After a short distance, the wall turns 90° and heads directly towards Gavel Gap. The official track essentially cuts the corner off the field by heading diagonally across it.

Although not surfaced, the track is easy to follow and pleasant to ride, until a well-surfaced gravel trail suddenly appears for no apparent reason. Following this trail soon leads to a gate at Gavel Gap, where beyond the gate, the trail leads invitingly off into the distance. Route-finding is now simplicity itself, as easy, downhill riding along the **Ribble Way** gives those weary leg muscles a well-earned rest.

The superb descent runs alongside the stream of Jam Sike, one of the main tributaries into Gayle Beck and thence into the embryonic River Ribble. From there, it grows into the mighty river that ultimately disgorges into the Irish Sea at Lytham.

Watch out for the conspicuous white farmhouse high up on the fellside in the distance ahead. This is Newby Head Farm, and that ominous-looking hill behind is where the PB heads next as it climbs up towards Great Knoutberry Hill (but thankfully not on this ride).

Beginning the descent from Gavel Gap

Rainwater trickling into the streams only a few metres to the north of Gavel Gap will have a very different journey; for this is the watershed of the Pennines and that extra few metres will dictate that their wanderings will take them down Snaizeholme and Widdale Becks, then into the River Ure, to end their journey as the Ouse, in the Humber Estuary on the east coast.

The fabulous descent continues, passing a rather incongruous concrete shed on the way, eventually to end at a farm gate opening out onto the **B6255** at Newby Head Gate with the road to Upper Dentdale going off more-or-less **SA**. A new section of off-road bridleway (complete with ford) has been created to cut off the corner rather than endure a 20m dogleg along the main road. (About 400m along the Dentdale road, a newly resurfaced bridleway leading steeply up onto Wold Fell will be passed on the right, a section of Route 8.)

5 A further 400m along the road a signposted bridleway heads off **L** (**Black Rake Road**). Early mountain bike guidebooks described this section of trail as 'deteriorating into a boggy morass'. However, extensive

More new bridleway, alongside the headwaters of the Ribble

Gayle Beck

resurfacing has taken place and now, even at the end of a long, wet winter, the trail is easily rideable with only an occasional squelchy hint of the quagmire that once prevailed here.

The Black Rake Road climbs steadily, but relatively gently, to a high point below **Blea Moor Moss**. It then turns a little to the **L** and begins its descent towards **High Gayle Farm**. Just above the farm, a junction is met where a very mossy signpost indicates the Dales Way footpath going off right. Ignore this and continue a little further downhill to another junction where the most prominent track turns sharp right towards the farm. The correct route is **SA**, dropping a little further downhill, through a rickety gate and following the wall on the right. After a few further metres of descent, the track swings back sharp **R** to run along (**an often muddy**) farm track and out onto the main drive up to High Gayle Farm, just on the downhill side of the gate. Turn **L** down the farm drive to meet the **B6255** where another **L** turn quickly returns to the start point at Gayle Beck Lodge.

Note To return to Ribblehead turn **R** along the **B6255** at this point and follow it back to the viaduct and transport home.

Bridge and blossom, Dentdale (photo: EA Bowness)

8 Arten Gill, Dent Head Viaduct and the Driving Road

START/FINISH	On the road between Dent Station and Garsdale Head Station **SD 779 880**
DISTANCE	15km (9½ miles)
OFF ROAD	11.5km (7¼ miles)
ON ROAD	3.5km (2¼ miles)
ASCENT	470m (1535ft)
TIME	2hrs 30mins–4hrs
OVERALL GRADING	■
MAP	OS Explorer OL2 Yorkshire Dales (Southern & Western areas)
PUBS	The Sportsman's Inn, Cowgill; or detour to the Moorcock Inn, Garsdale Head
CAFÉS	None on main route; detour to Dent
RAILWAY ACCESS	Dent Station on the Settle–Carlisle line (see below for directions to start)

75% OFF ROAD

The area above Dent Head has long been the scene of man's desperate fight against the harshest of elements in an attempt to earn a living. Lead, coal, lime, railways; all have been won from these barren hills and each process has left its own industrial legacy on the landscape. Time has softened the scars to give a fascinating glimpse into the brutally harsh lifestyle these pioneers must have endured. One legacy for our privileged generation is a network of packhorse trails, roads and bridleways, criss-crossing the high fells. The best of these have now been enhanced and extended to create a memorable trail that takes in the best of the scenery and some of the most spectacular gems of our industrial heritage. Treat this route with respect: these moorlands can be barren, the climbs are steep and the winds sometimes vicious.

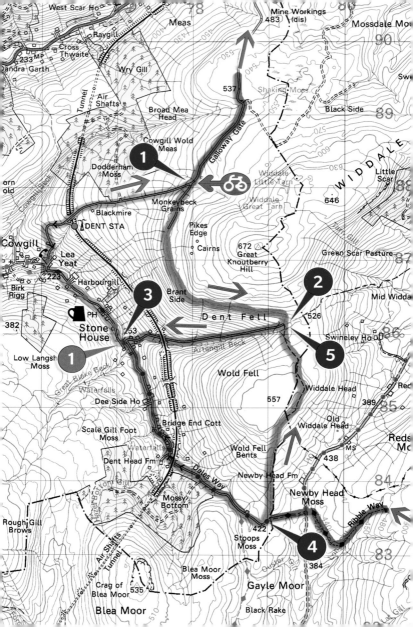

The start point point of the ride can be accessed via the lovely village of Dent. From the Sedbergh end, pass the village school (right) then enter a narrow, cobbled section of the main street. A little beyond the Sun Inn the road splits; take the **LH** branch. Continue downhill, between the church and village shop, then leave the village, cross-

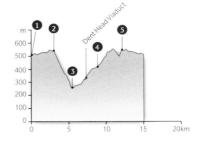

ing the River Dee by Church Bridge. Follow this fabulous valley road for 5.75km to the hamlet of **Cowgill**. At the far end of the houses, a right-angle bend in the road leads to the bridge at Lea Yeat; but just before the bridge a road **L** leads steeply uphill to **Dent Station**. This is the 'Coal Road'; coal was once mined in the dale, and the road from Cowgill to Garsdale consequently gained an industrial connotation that is totally at odds with the landscape today. Take this steeply ascending, narrow road; 800m of relentless ascent later the entrance to **Dent Station** will be found on the right. Continue to climb steeply uphill.

> **Note** If travelling by train, join the route at this point by turning **R** uphill from the station.

The trees of **Dodderham Moss** (left) indicate a merciful release from the worst of the climbing until, about 400m further along the road, a signposted and well-surfaced track, heading off to the **R** gently uphill, around the flanks of Great Knoutberry Hill, marks the starting point of the ride. A large gravel area around the gate gives adequate parking opportunities, and the views in every direction are an indication of what is to come on this fabulous ride.

DIRECTIONS

1 The track used at the start of this ride, commonly known as 'the Driving Road', is also the route of the PB as it climbs up from Newby Head Gate en route for Garsdale Head, and it provides lovely riding with superb views all around. All too soon, having crossed a couple of cobbled fords on the way, a downhill section leads to a sharp **RH** bend and a short descent to a gate and a T-junction of tracks. Arriving at the junction, the obvious downhill track **R** is the wonderful descent of **Arten Gill**.

Note Through a gate on the left a continuation of the Arten Gill track climbs gently out of sight, over the brow of the hill, to run alongside Lings Beck on its way down Widdale (**a very rocky, technical descent – not recommended**). Immediately on the other side of the gate, the newly graded track dropping into a boggy dip then climbing back up the hill (alongside a wall) straight ahead is the return route back to this point.

2 The gradient, gentle at first, soon begins to drop more steeply alongside the impressive streamway of Arten Gill. This is a superb descent! The track is newly repaired, the pace can be as fast as your nerve will allow and the views are stunning. **Take a little care as numerous drainage culverts are crossed**: the stone facing on some of these can be a little steep. However, other than that, the downhill run is broken only by the odd farm gate (and the occasional manic sheep).

Towards the bottom of the gill, the angle of descent eases as the impressive profile of the **Arten Gill Viaduct** draws into view. A final gate, alongside a curious, bell-shaped structure (once a limekiln?), gives access to the drive leading past **Stone House Farm** and then out to the tarmac road surface at Stone House Bridge.

ALTERNATIVE FINISH VIA DENT STATION

1 The route can be shortened considerably here, by crossing the bridge and continuing down-valley for about 1.5km, passing The Sportsman's Inn on the left, and continuing on to the next bridge at **Lea Yeat**. Cross Lea Yeat Bridge and take the road **SA**, leading steeply uphill, signposted for *Dent Station and Garsdale Head*. Eventually, after some killer climbing, the turn-off into Dent Station will be passed. Keep climbing up the hill ahead until you reach the starting point after 1.5km.

3 If the descent of Arten Gill has got you screaming for more turn **L** along the road, before crossing the bridge and heading up-valley. This road climbs steeply underneath the **Dent Head Viaduct**, and then continues a little more gently to head towards the main **B6255** (Hawes-to-Ingleton road), which it meets some 2km beyond the viaduct. However, about 500m before the road junction a prominent track (and *PB* signpost at a conspicuous double gate) will be found going off on the **L** of the road at the beginning of the steep climb up Wold Fell, rejoining the route of the PB.

4 Immediately through the gate, the well-surfaced track begins to climb steeply up Newby Head Field and Newby Head Pasture to another gate, with fine views behind of all Three Peaks. The area around this second gate can be muddy, as the trail continues (almost flat now) across a grassy area, to yet another gate leading into the lovely shallow valley beyond.

The view up Arten Gill – the descent is preferable!

The grassy surface has a track of sorts, which is easy to follow. At the end of the valley, this trail swings **L**, up a short climb over the shoulder of the hill then goes back **R** as it heads towards a descent into Swineley Cowm and the head of Arten Gill. Although the trail in this area is easy to follow, it is worth remembering that, just out of sight over the rise on the **L**, is a field boundary wall. The track and the wall converge until they meet at a wall corner. Wall and path now run side-by-side, down a short hill into a hollow. One or two areas on this descent are boggy, but can still be ridden with little difficulty. Drainage work was carried out in summer 2011 will no doubt have sorted out the problem. From the bottom of the descent a short, steep climb leads up to a gate giving access to the junction at the top of **Arten Gill**.

5 As this route is essentially the shape of a tennis racquet (the outward journey forming the handle), the return to the start point from here is back the way you originally came, through the gate on the **R** and up the short hill that follows. Another gate marks the end of the steeper climbing and a further 3km of easy riding, with stunning views, leads back to tarmac at the starting point.

To return to Dent Station a **L** turn, down the road will give an exhilarating descent back to the station entrance in 1.5km.

Descending into Cowgill, Dentdale

9 Garsdale to Dentdale via Dandra Garth

9

START/FINISH	Dandra Garth on the A684 at Garsdale **SD 752 897**
VIA ARTEN GILL	
DISTANCE	20.5km (12¾ miles)
OFF ROAD	9.75km (6 miles)
ON ROAD	10.75km (6¾ miles)
ASCENT	610m (2000ft)
ALTERNATIVE RETURN VIA DENT STATION	
DISTANCE	15.75km (9¾ miles)
OFF ROAD	3.5km (2¼ miles)
ON ROAD	12.25km (7½ miles)
ASCENT	550m (1800ft)
TIME	3–5hrs (both options)
OVERALL GRADING	▲
MAPS	OS Explorers OL2 Yorkshire Dales (Southern & Western areas), OL19 Howgill Fells & Upper Eden Valley
PUBS	The Moorcock Inn, Garsdale Head; The Sportsman's Inn, Cowgill
CAFÉS	None on main route; detour to Dent, Ingleton, Kirkby Stephen or Hawes
RAILWAY ACCESS	Garsdale Head Station or Dent Station on the Settle–Carlisle line (see below for directions to route)

The bridleway from Garsdale over to Dentdale via Black Hill could give a fabulous ride, but has been badly damaged by years of illegal activity by trail bikes. The ultimate effect of this abuse is an unrideable trail that is no use to anyone (including those who did the damage in the first place). Fortunately over the time since motor vehicles were banned from this bridleway the surface has begun to recover, but there are still some sections that will require the occasional push. The ride is included in this guide for two reasons: normal traffic will gradually improve the surface and help the trail to recover by regular usage; most of the bridleway is still in very rideable condition, and the circuit it creates is a lovely route with stunning situations.

The ride can be started from a number of locations, including the stations at Dent and Garsdale Head. To access the route from **Garsdale Head Station**, exit the station yard directly onto the road coming down from the Galloway Gate. Turn **R** (downhill) to pass under the railway bridge and continue down to the main **A684**. Follow the route description below from **East Clough** (Point 7), eventually turning **L** off the road to find the bridleway at **Dandra Garth**. To access the route from **Dent Station**, turn **L** down the road to join it at **Lea Yeat Bridge** and turn **L** (Point 3).

When travelling up-valley on the **A684** from Sedbergh towards Garsdale Head, a sharp **R** turn takes the road across the Clough river and an equally sharp bend to the **L** then leads into the main street through the hamlet of Garsdale. About 800m further up the valley, a layby will be found next to the river, just opposite the farm at **Dandra Garth**. Plenty of other

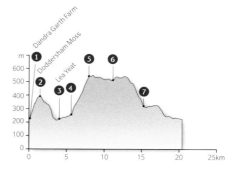

possibilities for parking exist nearby if this convenient lay-by is already occupied.

Directions

1 The farm at **Dandra Garth** is an ideal starting point for the ride. Once through the farm gate, an obvious bridleway track heads off through the farm past its attractive buildings and up into the woodland behind. The track

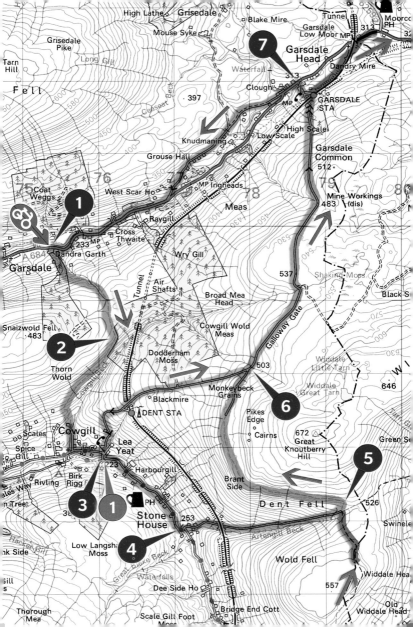

is well surfaced, but steep (and will get even steeper before the end of the wood is reached). Less than 400m further ahead, daylight is seen through the trees at a point where the forest track turns sharp right (continuing into the woodland). Here, the bridleway continues **SA**, climbing a few more metres up to a gate giving access onto open fellside.

Once through the gate, the increasingly steep hillside ahead looks daunting. However, the track essentially follows the wall running along the lower end of the field at a much more manageable gradient. Aiming for the wall corner just ahead, pick the easiest route through the initial boggy area around the gate. Where the wall turns sharp **L** look for a vague, raised terrace a few metres away from the wall that avoids the worst of the 'clag'. This terrace can then be followed, on a gently angled climb, until the deeply cut streamway of Blea Gill is encountered.

Route-finding now becomes simple as the streamway is followed up the hill, initially on the right bank, then crossing to climb past a marker post – steadily uphill – between the stream and the wall. The top of the main climb is reached surprisingly easily and, although some rutting will be found on the surface,

Thank goodness for bridges!

this section of trail can be ridden without much difficulty (by those who are fit enough!). This summit area of Black Hill is also named 'Black Hill Moss', so the next section of route should hold no surprises. Luckily some kind-hearted Samaritans have gone to a great deal of effort to build four bridges over the worst of the boggy areas, so this section now presents no major problems.

Looking back towards Dent Head Viaduct from Upper Dentdale (photo: EA Bowness)

Once over the last bridge aim for the wall corner just ahead, to the right of the woodland (drier ground will be found towards the right of the trail). The track away from the wall corner is obvious (keep between the wall and the woodland) but, in case of difficulty, a bridleway post conveniently marks the way on. It is the next section of trail that gives most disappointment on this route. What should be the start of a wonderful downhill run has been destroyed as the motorised brigade have been forced together through this narrow section of track. Deep ruts have formed, and parts of the trail are now virtually unrideable. This being said however, there are current moves to repair the worst of this damage, so conditions may have improved considerably by the time you reach this point.

2 The most damaged section of trail is found alongside the woodland of **Dodderham Moss** but luckily, once this particularly narrow section is over, conditions quickly improve. Past the end of the wood the trail enters a lovely walled lane with a pleasant, grassy surface and views down over **Cowgill Beck** in the gill to the left. Nice riding, with an occasional rutted section, leads along a classic walled drove road, high above Upper Dentdale with wonderful views over Whernside and Deepdale.

The grassy lane begins to drop steadily downwards towards **Cowgill**, until a steep, gated hairpin marks the beginning of the final, exciting descent into the valley bottom. This last section of trail has been resurfaced and provides a particularly pleasant end to a somewhat mixed descent. Follow the tarmac lane down over Dockra Bridge to meet the main valley road alongside the churchyard. A **L** turn here leads quickly up to **Lea Yeat Bridge** over the River Dee, with a lane heading off left up to Dent Station and Garsdale Head. It is now decision time!

ALTERNATIVE RETURN VIA DENT STATION

① The shorter route (turning **L**), leads very steeply up to **Dent Station**, then even further upwards along the Coal Road to rejoin the main route at point ⑥.

> About 1.5km beyond Dent Station a gravel lane comes in from the right and this is where those who take the main (highly recommended) route will come zooming down. The longer route adds 5km and 60m of extra climbing, but the riding and the views are worth every extra ounce of effort.

③ To continue on the main route turn **R** over the bridge then follow the road back **L** (up-valley) in a lovely setting alongside the River Dee. Soon, The Sportsman's Inn will be passed and, 500m further along, the road swings **L** to cross the river again at Stone House bridge.

④ Cross the bridge but immediately leave the road at this point by continuing **SA** along the access lane to a number of cottages and up towards the spectacular viaduct of Arten Gill. The tarmac lane runs out at a gate by an information board about the viaduct. Beyond the gate, a gravel lane climbs steeply at first, then more gently once the first bend is rounded. Easier climbing now leads up to (and underneath) the viaduct.

Now starts the ascent of Arten Gill, which, although looking rather fearsome from the bottom, is a long climb rather than a steep one (tackled in reverse on Route 8). 2km and three gates later should see you panting up to a T-junction on the top of the hill with gates to the left and straight ahead. The PB comes through the gate ahead and both routes now join. On reaching the top of **Arten Gill**, take the gate on the **L**; the track climbs steeply before turning sharp **L** and the gradient eases.

5 This is the Driving Road, an ancient drove road giving superlative riding in surroundings of exceptional beauty. Was the extra climbing worth it? Absolutely!

The surface of the Driving Road is excellent, gradient is kind and the views just keep on coming. As the track circles the flanks of **Great Knoutberry Hill**, vistas of Ingleborough change to those of Whernside, then down into Dentdale, round to Garsdale, the Howgills, Wild Boar Fell and the Mallerstang Valley. A superb panorama!

Arten Gill Viaduct from the Driving Road

6 Eventually, the Driving Road ends at tarmac about 1.5km above Dent Station on the Coal Road (where the shorter option rejoins the main route). The final few miles back to Garsdale are on tarmac but you are unlikely to meet many cars on this road. A number of short climbs rise up to the high point of the route on the appropriately named Windy Hill, before the road (now the **Galloway Gate**) begins its speedy descent into **Garsdale Head**.

An excitingly steep section leads down to the station buildings where the road passes under the railway and past a row of cottages. The homeward route leaves the PB at **Garsdale Head Station** by continuing down the road to meet the main Sedbergh-to-Hawse road (**A684**) at East Clough.

7 Turn **L** down the main road for a short distance, looking out for a minor road going **SA** at Clouch Cottage, where the **A684** turns sharp left. This is the 'Old Road' and it gives a pleasantly quiet alternative to the busy **A684**. Climbing briefly up above Hining Scar, pass a junction off to Grisedale (part of Route 10) before dropping pleasantly down Cock Brow and a reunion with the **A684** near Mill Bridge. A **R** turn here leads to a gentle meander alongside the Clough river for about 1.2km back towards **Dandra Garth Farm** at Garsdale.

A lovely day on Hellgill Wold

10 Lady Anne's Highway and the Mallerstang Valley

START/FINISH	Shotlock Tunnel **SD 788 940** or Moorcock Inn, Garsdale Head **SD 797 927**
MAP	OS Explorer OL19 Howgill Fells & Upper Eden Valley
PUBS	Moorcock Inn, Garsdale Head; or detour to the Black Bull in Nateby or to various in Kirkby Stephen or Hawes
CAFÉS	None on main route; detour to Kirkby Stephen or Hawes
RAILWAY ACCESS	Garsdale Head Station on the Settle–Carlisle line (see below for directions to Moorcock Inn)

There are choices galore on this ride, making it suitable for any ability level! For an easy (but impressive) family trip, try the short version, directly up to Hell Gill via Shaw Paddock Farm. Extend this to a classic day-trip by opting for the newly created bridleway directly up the hill from Garsdale Head. For a tough ride that will really push stamina levels try the full route from Cotterdale to The Thrang, returning along the valley road before setting off across Dandry Mire to finish with the Grisedale Common loop. This last alternative (which can be added onto any of the previous routes) will really test your resolve as you pass the starting point (and pub) to begin the final section. Are your legs and willpower up to the ultimate test?

From **Garsdale Head Station**, exit the station yard directly onto the unclassified road coming down from the Galloway Gate. Turn **R** here (downhill) to pass under the railway bridge and continue down to the main **A684**. A **R** turn along the road leads to the Moorcock Inn road junction after 1.2km.

Off-road alternative: almost immediately after turning **R** out of the station area (but on the downhill side of the railway bridge) watch out on the **R** for a new bridleway that runs directly in front of a terrace of railway cottages.

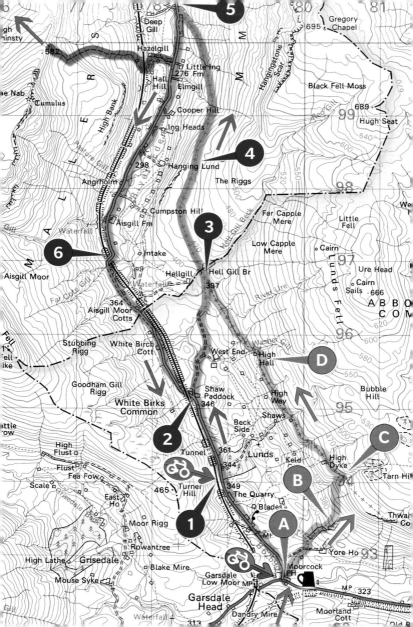

The track initially runs alongside the railway, before crossing underneath it at **Dandry Mire Viaduct**. The surfaced track then runs across an area of boggy ground, to exit onto the A684, just uphill from the Moorcock Inn and the start of the rides.

To find the starting point for the ride, follow any convenient route up to **Garsdale Head** and the junction of the A684 and the B6259 at the Moorcock Inn. Convenient parking can be found around this junction and at numerous points along the B6259 between the Moorcock Inn and the farm at **Shaw Paddock**. Parking nearer Shaw Paddock Farm will reduce the overall mileage a little but, for longer routes, a start point nearer the junction would be more convenient. For this reason the short route is described as starting from a small, gravel lay-by about 1.5km down the B6259 from the Moorcock Inn, opposite a (now largely felled and re-planted) wood near the Shotlock Tunnel.

Fine riding on Lady Anne's Highway

Short route

START/FINISH	Opposite the wood near the Shotlock Tunnel **SD 788 940**
DISTANCE	14km (8¾ miles)
OFF ROAD	5.75km (3½ miles)
ON ROAD	8.25km (5¼ miles)
ASCENT	275m (900ft)
TIME	1hr 30mins–3hrs
OVERALL GRADING	●

40%
OFF ROAD

Directions

1 Continue down the **B6259**, away from the **Garsdale Head** junction. Unfortunately, the route begins immediately with a short, steep climb. Once on top of the hill the entrance to the Shotlock Tunnel will be seen over the wall to the left and the road begins a pleasant downhill section to meet the buildings of **Shaw Paddock Farm** after about 800m.

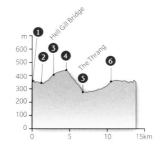

2 Immediately past Shaw Paddock the road swings left to pass under a railway bridge. A few yards **before** the bridge, however, a bridleway sign points into the main farm entrance (on the **RH** side of the road) then immediately through a farm gate onto a gravel-surfaced farm track. The track heads across the valley bottom before crossing a stream via an attractive stone bridge. This stream is the infant **River Ure** and its waters will eventually join the mighty Ouse as it flows out into the North Sea at Humberside.

Immediately over the bridge the track splits (the right branch heads off to buildings at Low and High, **West End**). Take the **L** branch to begin a long but steady climb up the hill towards Hell Gill Bridge. The climb is not particularly arduous as it crosses the Ure again at Green Bridge before meeting a junction with another track coming in from the right (this track is both the official route of the PB and the longer version of Lady Anne's Highway, along which those choosing either of the alternative starting points will be found haring down, grinning broadly!). Both tracks unite at this point to head off towards the prominent patch of trees, just ahead at **Hell Gill Bridge**.

③ The stream running through Hell Gill is the embryonic River Eden, which flows out into the Solway Firth, just beyond Carlisle. A matter of metres north or south from this point will dictate whether that falling raindrop becomes part of the North Sea or the Irish Sea: that short climb from the road has propelled you up to the watershed of the Pennines. Pass through the gate at the far side of Hell Gill Bridge and begin the gentle climb up Hellgill Wold. Following the wall on the left ensures that navigation is simple until, after about 1.5km, the wall turns away from the track at a truly spectacular viewpoint marked by an equally impressive sculpture, 'Water Cut', by the artist Mary Bourne.

④ This provides a convenient resting place to admire the views before beginning the wonderful descent immediately ahead. Over 2km of downhill bliss on a good gravel surface, with the odd ford and drainage ditch to focus the attention. A gate eventually ends the fun as an exit is made onto the `B6259` just south of the large B&B farmhouse at **The Thrang**.

⑤ From this point turn **L** to head up-valley along the road. Although the `B6259` is the main road along the Mallerstang Valley, it cannot be described as a busy thoroughfare. However, on weekends this is a popular route for strings of motorbikes en route to their pre-arranged meeting points.

From this route a tantalising bridleway is visible running along the eastern side of the valley, linking farms at Elmgill and Hanging Lund before joining the valley road again at Aisgill Moor Cottages. This bridleway then crosses the road and continues up the western side, passing High Shaw Paddock on the way up to Grisedale Common. This may look tempting as a return route, but is not recommended. The bridleway is very difficult to follow through deep bracken; the gates are rarely opened and the tracks mainly unrideable.

The first farm drive on the right leads across the river to High Dolphinsty and this is where the PB is left behind. The valley road climbs steadily, but not too steeply, past farms at **Angerholme** and **Aisgill** before crossing over the railway at Cotegill Bridge.

Wild Boar Fell from Upper Mallerstang (photo: EA Bowness)

6 From the bridge, continue for just under 1km until the road goes back under the railway at **Shaw Paddock Farm** (where the outward route began its climb up towards Hell Gill Bridge). A short but steep climb up Shotlock Hill follows before the gradient begins to drop downwards again to return to the start point at the wood near Shotlock Tunnel. The `B6259` continues onwards to lead back to the junction beside the Moorcock Inn.

ALTERNATIVE DIRECT START FROM THE MOORCOCK INN VIA COBBLES PLANTATION

START/FINISH	Moorcock Inn, Garsdale Head **SD 797 927**
DISTANCE	18km (11 miles)
OFF ROAD	9.25km (5¾ miles)
ON ROAD	8.75km (5¼ miles)
ASCENT	370m (1201ft)
TIME	2hrs 30mins–4hrs
OVERALL GRADING	▪

This follows a new section of bridleway constructed to link the PB with the existing right of way known as Lady Anne's Highway, which will not appear on current (2012) OS maps.

DIRECTIONS

A Facing the Moorcock Inn, the pub car park will be found to the left of the buildings, alongside the `B6259`. Just beyond the car park a new signposted track will be found going off **R**, across the moorland towards Cobbles Plantation and the driveway up to **Yore House Farm**. Follow this track until it meets the farm drive and a bridge across the infant River Ure. Once across the bridge, do not pass through the farm gate ahead, but take the track that bears **L** alongside the riverbank and heads up towards the trees at Cobbles Plantation.

The direct climb goes through the gate on the left of the trees

B Immediately beyond the trees, another track turns off **R** through a gate and begins to head steeply uphill, alongside the plantation. At the top of the first section of woodland, the track turns sharp right and crosses a small stream. Immediately before the stream however, another track, identified by a wooden *PB* signpost, bears off **L**, uphill, across the moorland.

The track keeps immediately to the left of a small stream, climbing steadily all the while. A line of wooden posts help guide the way as the indistinct track heads for the opposite field boundary some way ahead. As more height is gained, a small clump of trees will draw into view, by a significantly larger stream (Johnston Gill). On reaching Johnston Gill, turn sharp **R** and climb more steeply towards a wall on the top of the hill. Just to the left of a ruined limekiln a gate gives access to an obvious track on the other side of the wall.

C This is Lady Anne's Highway (also known as the **High Way**), which should be followed to the **L**, passing the abandoned buildings at **High Dyke** after a short distance. Both riding and navigation are delightfully easy, the only difficulties being a couple of deep fords that can become slippery in wet conditions, and a short, cobbled stairway, which those of a nervous disposition may choose to walk down.

D More abandoned buildings are passed immediately before the ford at **High Hall** and, just under 1.5km further along, a prominent farm track will be found climbing up the hillside from the left. This is the short route coming up from **Shaw Paddock Farm** and both routes now unite to continue towards the distinctive clump of trees marking **Hell Gill Bridge**, just ahead. Now continue from point **3** of the short route description.

Note The track down to Shaw Paddock Farm can provide a convenient escape route from Lady Anne's Highway. The track is downhill, easy to follow and pleasant to ride. The farmyard gives direct access onto the `B6259`, which can be followed to the **L** (**S** to reach the Moorcock Inn after 3.2km of easy riding.

I did warn you that the fords could be slippery!

Alternative start from the Moorcock Inn via the Cotterdale Loop

Start/Finish	Moorcock Inn, Garsdale Head **SD 797 927**
Distance	25.25km (15¾ miles)
Off road	11.75km (7¼ miles)
On road	13.5km (8½ miles)
Ascent	565m (1860ft)
Time	3hrs 15mins–5hrs 30mins
Overall grading	■

45%
OFF ROAD

This longer alternative start adds about 9km and 195m of additional ascent to the alternative direct start via Cobbles Plantation. It is worth the extra effort, however, just for the experience of riding this historic trail in its entirety.

Directions

A2 Begin by riding past the front of the Moorcock Inn, heading down the `A684` towards Hawes. **This road demands a little caution** because it can be quite busy during the summer months.

B2 After a couple of kilometres of descent, the River Ure is crossed at **Thwaite Bridge** and the road begins to climb again. Less than 1.5km further along Collier Holme Farm will be found on the right of the road, directly opposite the minor road heading off up to **Cotterdale**.

C2 Immediately alongside the `A684` at this point (**L**), Lady Anne's Highway heads back the way just travelled, steeply up the flanks of **Cotter Riggs** on a newly repaired gravel surface. The transformation of this track, from a quagmire with impassable ruts, has been a remarkable achievement for all involved. A pleasant gravel riding surface gives an easy ascent until steeper gradients are encountered further up the hill. Resurfacing has made the track a rather conspicuous feature across the fellside but this will soon

One of the fords on Lady Anne's Highway

mellow with the passage of time and enables an easy-to-follow climb directly up the face of Cotter Riggs, heading for a gate, high up in the distance at **Cotter End**.

D2 Once through the gate, a further short climb passes an abandoned limekiln. Relax now (the climbing is all but over) and enjoy superb views as Lady Anne's Highway continues, immediately alongside a wall on the left. The bleak moorland on the right at this point is **Thwaite Bridge Common**, contained by a single, drystone boundary wall at the far end. Watch carefully for this marker heading off up the hillside to the right because it is a useful indicator that the direct start from the Moorcock Inn will link up with the High Way in about 400m through a farm gate on the left (marked by a *PB* signpost). Keep ahead along the **High Way**, as described for the direct start, points **C** and **D**, to come to Hell Gill Bridge, where you continue from point **3** of the short route description.

The Grisedale Loop extension

Start/Finish	Moorcock Inn, Garsdale Head
	SD 797 927
Distance	8.25km (5 miles)
Off road	3.5km (2 miles)
On road	4.75km (3 miles)
Ascent	220m (720ft)
Time	45mins–1hr 30mins
Overall grading	■

If – having completed one of the other rides – a further challenge tempts you, add the following loop to your day out.

Directions

1. Looking out of the Moorcock Inn car park, with the pub buildings on the left, a bridleway gate will be found on the opposite side of the road. This new section of bridleway cuts off the corner between the **B6259** and the **A684**, thereby avoiding the ride along a potentially busy road. On arriving at the **A684 cross with care** to find another bridleway gate leading to an extension of the bridleway across the charmingly named **Dandry Mire**. Easy riding leads to another bridleway gate alongside the railway embankment.

   A short downhill section follows, where yet another gate leads to a continuation of the track as it passes under the Dandry Mire Viaduct. More easy riding follows alongside the railway, crossing a wooden bridge en route to a terrace of railway cottages alongside **Garsdale Head Station**. At the end of the cottages, the new bridleway exits onto tarmac just downhill from the station. A **R** turn here (downhill) leaves the official route of the PB and drops down to meet the **A684** at East Clough.

2. Turn **L** down the main road for a short distance, looking out for a minor road going off **SA** at Clouch Cottage, where the **A684** turns sharp left. This is the 'Old Road', which gives a pleasantly quiet alternative to the busy **A684**. Climbing briefly up above Hining Scar, the Old Road reaches a junction off to

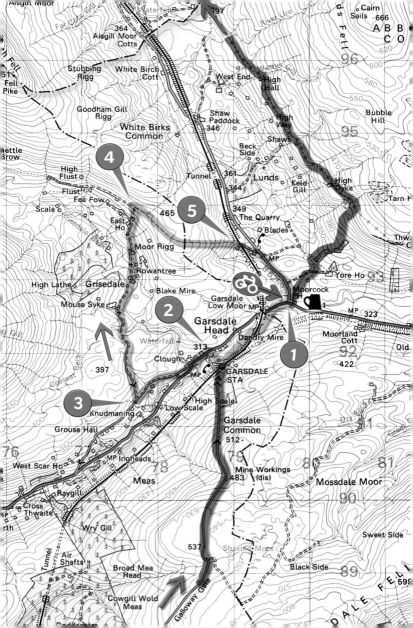

The new trail across Dandry Mire

the **R**, which heads upwards into the little-visited and largely unknown valley of Grisedale.

③ The first section of road is particularly steep but soon eases to give pleasant riding as the lovely view into the Grisedale Valley begins to open up ahead. A welcome downhill section crosses Stony Gill at Double Hale Bridge before another downhill run leads to a gate at the entrance drive to Mouse Syke Farm. The Grisedale Road now begins a long, steady climb, passing buildings at **Rowantree** and **Moor Rigg** before reaching the end of the tarmac road just beyond the buildings at **East House Farm**. Arriving at the farm, a gate and cattle grid mark the start of another short, steep section that leads up to a junction of unsurfaced tracks at the bottom of Grisedale Common.

④ Turn **R** along the obvious track for a short distance to where a signposted bridleway bears off left across the uninviting looking fellside (not recommended). Ignore this and follow the main farm track, which follows the wall on the right and gives easy riding in very pleasant surroundings. After a short distance the track becomes less clear on the ground and begins to bear away from the wall. Keep more-or-less **SA** at this point, aiming for the twin 'fingers' of a ladder stile on the horizon, until the wall on the other side of the field draws fully into view and a gate alongside the ladder stile becomes evident.

On reaching the other side of the field, pass through the gate to find another field wall (on the left this time) dropping down the hillside ahead. The path across the heather-clad hillside ahead is not always that easy to spot initially: looking over to the left, a gate will be found at the very top of the field wall. Head over to that gate and look carefully in the undergrowth for a narrow track, heading downhill through the heather. It is worth persevering here because the track gives a very pleasant, meandering, single-track descent, gradually bearing away from the wall towards the railway buildings and footbridge at the bottom of the hill.

5 Approaching the railway line, the track heads across to the railway cottage where gates give access to a pedestrian crossing over the line and a continuation of the farm drive out onto the `B6259`. A **R** turn along the road then leads back to the Moorcock Inn junction after 800m of easy descent and the end of a very pleasant extension.

Moorland Pony, Grisedale (photo: EA Bowness)

Any idea where we are?

11 Ravenstonedale, Pendragon Castle and High Dolphinsty

11

START/FINISH	Road junction on the A683 with Bowber Head at Crooks Beck Bridge **NY 742 028**
DISTANCE	17.5km (11 miles)
OFF ROAD	9.5km (6 miles)
ON ROAD	8km (5 miles)
ASCENT	520m (1700ft)
TIME	4–6hrs
OVERALL GRADING	▲
MAP	OS Explorer OL19 Howgill Fells & Upper Eden Valley
PUBS	The Fat Lamb, Ravenstonedale; or detour to The Black Swan or The King's Head, Ravenstonedale
CAFÉS	None en route; detour to Lune Springs Garden Centre, Newbiggin-on-Lune, or to various in Kirkby Stephen
RAILWAY ACCESS	Kirkby Stephen Station on the Settle–Carlisle line (see below for directions to start)

55%
OFF ROAD

This is a truly memorable ride, with superb viewpoints in a rarely visited area. It is also one that must be treated with respect – the climb out of Mallerstang is steep and unrelenting, while the flanks of Wild Boar Fell are an unpleasant place to be in bad weather conditions. However, route-finding is easy, the tracks are well maintained and the descents a delight! It's a little gem that doesn't give up its charms without some considerable effort.

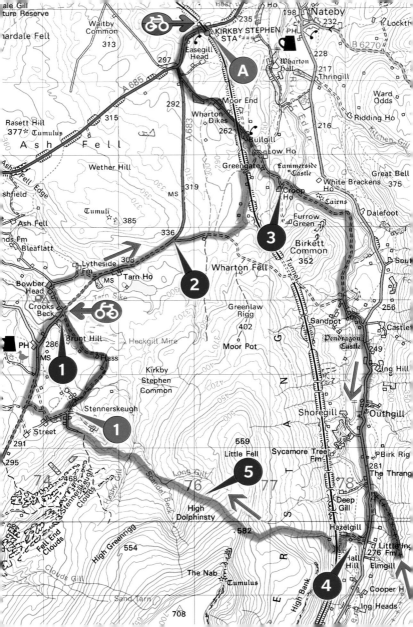

To find the start point for the ride, follow the A683 Sedbergh-to-Kirkby Stephen road to where Townhead Lane goes off to Ravenstonedale (immediately alongside the Fat Lamb Inn). Numerous parking possibilities exist in the area around the Fat Lamb or, even better, immediately alongside the A683 between the Fat Lamb turn-off and the hamlet of **Bowber Head** a little further towards Kirkby Stephen.

Alternative start

· ·

A To pick up the route from **Kirkby Stephen Station** turn **L** onto the A685, immediately passing under the railway and climbing up the hill ahead. After 800m take the A683 towards Sedbergh, then 200m further along, branch off **L** onto Bullgill Lane (signposted *No Through Road*). Follow Bullgill Lane, pleasantly downhill, to pick up the main route at **Low House Farm** after 1.5km.

Directions

1 The route begins by following the A683 towards Kirkby Stephen and taking the minor road off **L** to Bowber Head, alongside **Crooks Beck**. Once in **Bowber Head**, climb a short rise to a T-junction with a lane coming in from Ravenstonedale. Turn **R** to join up with the A683 again after a short distance (and just before meeting **Tarn House Farm**).

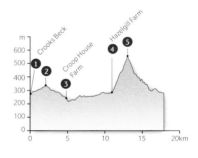

Past the farm, climb the hill ahead with nice views of the tarn on the right until, once on easier ground at the top of the hill, take a minor lane to the **R** signposted *Mallerstang*.

2 This is Tommy Road, which, if followed to its conclusion, would lead to Pendragon Castle (visited later on the route) in the lovely, and often forgotten, Mallerstang Valley. Tommy Road drops downhill and soon crosses a cattle grid. Immediately over the cattle grid, the first of three bridleways is met. Take the third of these, which heads off to the **L**, away from the road at the bottom of the long hill, and gives a short, pleasant downhill run alongside a wall (left).

The good track soon leads to a junction where an alternative route goes off to the right, over the brow of the hill. The more obvious farm track continues **SA** along a very wide, walled lane, climbing gently to a gate on the **R**. The gate allows direct access onto a bridge over the Settle–Carlisle line at **Greengate**. Once over the railway, the farm track continues downwards to meet Bullgill Lane just above the buildings of **Low House Farm**. Turn **R** here, down the tarmac lane.

Note This is the point where the alternative start from the railway station joins up with the main route.

Pendragon Castle bedecked in springtime harebells

3 The lane drops steeply down to **Croop House Farm** at the bottom of the hill. The farmhouse will be on the right as the farmyard is entered, so look out on the **L** for an obvious farm track, which drops down the small hill **L**, towards the river. This track (a public byway) turns sharp **R** as it meets a wall. A farm gate then gives access to a continuation of the byway along the banks of the infant **River Eden**. Having crossed a small bridge head upstream, with the river left, along a muddy byway, obviously frequented by an assortment of motor vehicles.

The track heads directly towards the road running up the Mallerstang Valley,with the River Eden left. As the byway and road get closer the byway turns sharp **R** and begins to climb steadily up the lower flanks of **Birkett Common**. The track gains some height before dropping back down into Black Hill Hollow then climbs steeply up again to meet the road at a cattle grid. This is the bottom end of Tommy Road; follow it downhill to the **L** to reach the Mallerstang Valley road (**B6259**) at a junction, with the atmospheric ruins of **Pendragon Castle** on the right (free entry).

Continue off to the **R**, up-valley, towards the small hamlet of **Outhgill**. The road climbs steadily for about 1 km, past a farmhouse called **The Thrang** on the right, then drops down a small dip to meet a prominent track/bridleway joining the road on the left (the lower end of Lady Anne's Highway and the route of the PB). At this junction cast an eye over to that great chunk of limestone to the right: that ominous-looking hill is Wild Boar Fell, encountered later on the route. Fortunately the route takes one of the lower passes to the right of the main peak, but it's still a tough proposition!

To reach the beginning of the climb up to High Dolphinsty rejoin the official route of the PB and continue up-valley, along the road, for a few hundred metres, to a point where a farm track (signposted bridleway) heads off **R** to **Hazelgill Farm**.

4 Pass through the farm gate; just before the farmhouse is reached a track goes off **L** towards barns and farm machinery. Take this track, which quickly turns **R** up by the main farm buildings, following some very small bridleway posts. Once past the buildings the lane is easy to follow as it runs uphill to the **L**, alongside the railway embankment. After a short, steep climb, the track passes under the railway, gains a little more height, then hairpins back on itself, climbing steadily all the while.

Just after a ford near a stone barn, the track turns sharp **L** to run alongside a small stream cascading down the hillside. Eventually a farm gate is reached and, after a steep little pull, the gradient relents a little. A good gravel track

Journey's end! Beginning the spectacular descent from High Dolphinsty towards Street

is followed until the next steep section arrives, at which point the track abruptly ends. Continue more-or-less **SA**, up a small rise, where a line of bridleway posts will then become evident. Follow these posts to quickly find a more obvious track heading up to the correct dip in the skyline.

5 On reaching the summit look through the small gate on the right to see the trail disappearing off down the other side. Mile after mile of quality trail – and all of it downhill. Route-finding is not a problem here: there is only one track and it is in excellent condition, giving fantastic riding with minimal effort. A couple of fords give a brief respite to the downhill charge until a junction is met just above the buildings of **Stennerskeugh Farm**. Ignore the track dropping down towards the farm buildings and follow the higher trail as it swings round to the **L**. Shortly after, a **steep, rocky section** leads down to a tarmac lane at **Street** and this should be followed to the **R**, downhill again, to a junction. A **L** turn here (the official PB route) can be followed out to the main road (**A683**). Turn **R** along the road to return to the start.

ALTERNATIVE FINISH

. . . .

1 A more interesting route to return to the start point can be taken by turning **R** at the junction below **Street**. The lane quickly leads to **Stennerskeugh Farm** where a signposted bridleway leads along to a substantial ford. Cross the ford to quickly meet a junction of tracks. The right-hand track goes through a gate and up to some modern barns. Ignore this, however, and take the **LH** route, which crosses another wet area, then climbs over an ancient stone bridge. The track climbs a little, and then continues to rise more gently, alongside a wall on the left. The peaty surface gives pleasant riding over numerous small bumps and rises, all the time following the wall. After a short distance, the wall turns 45° left and drops down a small hill.

Follow the wall as it heads through a boggy area down towards the farm buildings at **Flass**. Just beyond the farm garden, a small gate (with bridleway marker) gives access to a paddock with a corresponding gate on the far side. Beyond the second gate, a short section of farm track leads out onto the road at the front of the farm. Turn **R** along the tarmac lane to quickly meet the **A683** in less than 1km. The junction with the **A683** is directly opposite the lane up to **Bowber Head** at the start of the route. Note that the Fat Lamb is a tantalisingly short distance along the road to the left!

To return to **Kirkby Stephen Station**, follow the directions at the start of this route as far as the **Tommy Road** and take the first bridleway **L** across the fell to Bullgill Lane. Turn **L** along Bullgill Lane and retrace your tracks back to the station after 1.5km.

Appendix A
Route summary tables

DISTANCES BETWEEN KEY POINTS			
SECTION 1 **THE MARY TOWNELEY LOOP**			
Summit to Hurstwood 6–8hrs			
From	**To**	**Distance**	**Time**
Summit	Bottomley	2.5km (1½ miles)	30–45mins
Bottomley	Lumbutts	3.75km (2¼ miles)	1–1hr 15mins
Lumbutts	Charlestown	6.75km (4¼ miles)	1–1hr 20mins
Charlestown	Jack Bridge	3km (2 miles)	1–1hr 15mins
Jack Bridge	Gorple Lower Reservoir	6.5km (4 miles)	1–1hr 20mins
Gorple Lower Reservoir	Widdop Reservoir	2.5km (1½ miles)	30–45mins
Widdop Reservoir	Hurstwood	6km (3¾ miles)	1–1hr 20mins

SECTION 2 THE LANCASHIRE LINK			
Hurstwood to Barnoldswick 5–7hrs			
From	**To**	**Distance**	**Time**
Hurstwood	Wycoller	13.5km (8½ miles)	2–3hrs
Wycoller	Kelbrook	9.5km (6 miles)	2–2hrs 40mins
Kelbrook	Barnoldswick	5.5km (3½ miles)	1–1hr 20mins

Barnoldswick to Long Preston 3–5hrs			
From	**To**	**Distance**	**Time**
Barnoldswick	Gisburn	10.75km (6¾ miles)	1–1hr 30mins
Gisburn	Paythorne	6.5km (4 miles)	45mins–1hr 15mins
Paythorne	Halton West	3.5km (2¼ miles)	30–45mins
Halton West	Long Preston	6km (3¾ miles)	45mins–1hr 30mins

DISTANCES BETWEEN KEY POINTS			
SECTION 2 THE YORKSHIRE DALES			
Long Preston to Horton 7–9hrs			
From	To	Distance	Time
Long Preston	Settle	6km (3¾ miles)	1–1hr 20mins
Settle	Stainforth	5.5km (3½ miles)	1hr 10mins–1hr 30mins
Stainforth	Feizor	6.5km (4 miles)	1hr 15mins–1hr 30mins
Feizor	Austwick	3km (1¾ miles)	20–30mins
Austwick	Clapham	4km (2½ miles)	30–40mins
Clapham	Selside	9.25km (5¾ miles)	1hr 45mins–2hr 15mins
Selside	Horton	7.5km (4¾ miles)	1–1hr 15mins

Horton to Garsdale 4hrs 30mins–6hrs 30mins			
From	To	Distance	Time
Horton	Newby Head Gate	13.5km (8½ miles)	3–4hrs
Newby Head Gate	Dent Station	6.5km (4 miles)	50min–1hr 30mins
Dent Station	Garsdale Head	6.5km (4 miles)	40mins–1hr

Garsdale to Ravenstonedale 3–5hrs			
From	To	Distance	Time
Garsdale Head	The Thrang	9.25km (5¾ miles)	1–1hr 30mins
The Thrang	Street	6.5km (4 miles)	1hr 20mins–2hrs 30mins
Street	The Fat Lamb	3km (1¾ miles)	20–30mins
The Fat Lamb	Ravenstonedale	3km (1¾ miles)	20–30mins

Note These distances may not exactly match those given in the relevant section of the guide. This reflects the fact that a short detour will be necessary to visit those villages that are located just off the official route (such as Clapham, Austwick, Ribblehead and so on).

SECTION 3 – DAY LOOPS OFF THE PENNINE BRIDLEWAY

No.	Title	Overall grade	Start/Finish	Distance	Ascent	Time
1	The Settle Loop	■	Settle Market Square (SD 820 637)	16km (10 miles)	510m (1675ft)	2hrs 30mins–4hrs
2	Feizor, Wharfe and Catrigg Force	● ■	Buck Haw Brow (SD 796 658)	12km (8 miles) 21km (13 miles)	250m (815ft) 555m 1825ft)	1hr 30mins–3hrs 2hrs 30mins–4hrs
3	Clapham, Crummack Dale and Feizor	■	Clapham, main car park (SD 745 692)	18.5km (11½ miles)	465m (1525ft)	2hrs 30mins–4hrs
4	Horton-in-Ribblesdale, Helwith Bridge and Sulber Nick	●	Horton-in-Ribblesdale, main car park (SD 788 746)	17.5km (11 miles)	335m (1100ft)	2hrs 30mins–4hrs
5	Ribblehead to Ling Gill and Horton-in-Ribblesdale	▲	Junction of the B6255 and B6479 at Ribblehead Viaduct (SD 765 792)	25.75km (16 miles) 27km (16¾ miles)	564m (1850ft) 657m (2156ft)	3hrs 30mins–5hrs
6	Ribblehead to Dentdale via the Craven Way	▲	Junction of the B6255 and B6479 at Ribblehead Viaduct (SD 765 792)	25.75km (16 miles)	655m (2155ft)	4–6hrs

No.	Route		Start point	Distance	Ascent	Time
7	Cam High Road and the Ribble Way	■	Gayle Beck Lodge on the B6255 near Newby Head Gate (SD 791 814)	15km (9¼ miles)	335m (1100ft)	2–4hrs
8	Arten Gill, Dent Head Viaduct and the Driving Road	■	On the road between Dent Station and Garsdale Head Station (SD 779 880)	15km (9½ miles)	470m (1535ft)	2hrs 30mins–4hrs
9	Garsdale to Dentdale via Dandra Garth	◀	Dandra Garth on the A684 at Garsdale (SD 752 897)	20.5km (12¾ miles) 15.5km (9½ miles)	610m (2000ft) 550m (1800ft)	3–5hrs
10	Lady Anne's Highway and the Mallerstang Valley	●	Opposite the wood near the Shotlock Tunnel (SD 788 940)	14km (8¾ miles)	275m (900ft)	1hr 30mins–3hrs
		■	Moorcock Inn, Garsdale Head (SD 797 927)	18km (11 miles)	370m (1201ft)	2hrs 30mins–4hrs
		■	Cotterdale Loop	25.25km (15½ miles)	565m (1860ft)	3hrs 15mins–5hrs 30mins
		■	Griesdale Loop extension	8.25km (5 miles)	220m (720ft)	45mins–1hr 30mins
11	Ravenstonedale, Pendragon Castle and High Dolphinsty	◀	Road junction on the A683 with Bowber Head at Crooks Beck Bridge (NY 742 028)	17.5km (11 miles)	520m (1700ft)	4–6hrs

Appendix B
Local facilities

| | | SECTION 1 THE MARY TOWNELEY LOOP | | | | | | | | | |
| | | Summit to Hurstwood | | | | | | | | | |
Location	Shop	Campsite	Bunk House	B&B	Pub	Cycle Shop	TIC	Café	PO	Train Station	Hostel
Summit										*	
Bottomley										*	
Lumbutts		✓		✓							✓
Charlestown**	✓			✓	✓	✓	✓	✓	✓	*	✓
Jack Bridge		✓		✓	✓			✓	✓		
Gorple Lower Reservoir					✓						

* This area is served by the Caldervale line: stations at Todmorden, Hebden Bridge, Walsden and Littleborough

** Facilities available in Hebden Bridge (2.8km off the main route)

SECTION 2
THE LANCASHIRE LINK

Hurstwood to Barnoldswick

Location	Shop	Campsite	Bunk House	B&B	Pub	Cycle Shop	TIC	Café	PO	Train Station	Youth Hostel
Wycoller							✓	✓			
Kelbrook	✓	✓		✓					✓		
Barnoldswick	✓			✓	✓	✓	✓	✓	✓		✓

Barnoldswick to Long Preston

Location	Shop	Campsite	Bunk House	B&B	Pub	Cycle Shop	TIC	Café	PO	Train Station	Youth Hostel
Gisburn	✓			✓	✓			✓	✓		
Paythorne					✓						

SECTION 2
THE YORKSHIRE DALES

Long Preston to Horton

Location	Shop	Campsite	Bunk House	B&B	Pub	Cycle Shop	TIC	Café	PO	Train Station	Youth Hostel
Long Preston	✓	✓		✓	✓				✓	✓	
Settle	✓	✓	✓	✓	✓	✓	✓	✓	✓	✓	
Stainforth	✓	✓		✓	✓				✓		
Feizor				✓				✓			
Austwick	✓		✓	✓	✓				✓		
Clapham	✓			✓	✓				✓	✓	

	Horton to Garsdale Head						
Horton	✓	✓	✓		✓	✓	
Ribblehead	✓	✓				✓	✓
Dent Station		✓					✓
Dentdale	✓	✓			✓	✓	
	Garsdale Head to Ravenstonedale						
Garsdale Head	✓	✓				✓	✓
Outhgill		✓					
Street	✓	✓					
The Fat Lamb	✓	✓					
Ravenstonedale	✓	✓				✓	
Kirkby Stephen	✓	✓	✓	✓	✓	✓	✓

Approaching Hurstwood reservoir from Cant Clough
(Section 1)

Upland Pasture, Newby Head
(Section 3 Route 7; photo: EA Bowness)

Appendix C
Useful contacts

TOURIST INFORMATION OFFICES

Burnley TIC
Tel: 01282 477210
Email: tic@Burnley.gov.uk

Pendle Gateway Visitor Centre
Tel: 01282 856186
Email: DiscoverPendle@pendle.gov.uk

Wycoller Park Information Centre
Tel: 01282 870254

Barnoldswick TIC
Tel: 01282 666704

Settle TIC
Tel: 01729 825192
Email: settle@ytbtic.co.uk

Horton-in-Ribblesdale TIC
Tel: 01729 860333
Email: horton@ytbtic.co.uk

Sedbergh TIC
Tel: 01539 620125
Email: tic@sedbergh.org.uk

Kirkby Stephen TIC
Tel: 01768 371199
Email: ks.tic@eden.gov.uk

LOCAL ACCIDENT AND EMERGENCY DEPARTMENTS

Royal Oldham Hospital
Rochdale Road, Oldham
Tel: 0161 624 0420

Calderdale Royal Hospital
Salterhebble, Halifax
Tel: 01422 357171

Royal Blackburn Hospital
Haslingden Road, Blackburn
Tel: 01254 263555

Airedale General Hospital
Skipton Road, Steeton, Keighley
Tel: 01535 652511

Royal Lancaster Infirmary
Ashton Road, Lancaster
Tel: 01524 65944

Mountain bikers below Pen-y-ghent
(Section 3 Route 1; photo: EA Bowness)

Appendix D
Accommodation

MARY TOWNELEY LOOP

Summit
The Moorcock Inn, Littleborough
Tel: 01706 378156
www.themoorcockinn.co.uk

Hollingworth Lake Caravan and Campsite
Tel: 01706 378661

Mankinholes
Mankinholes Youth Hostel
Tel: 01706 812340
www.yha.org.uk

Gorple/Widdop
The Pack Horse Inn
Tel: 01422 842803
www.thepackhorse.org

THE LANCASHIRE LINK

Wycoller
Oaklands B&B
Tel: 01282 865893
www.oaklands-b-and-b.co.uk

Sough/Barnoldswick
Craven Heifer
Tel: 01282 843 007
www.thecravenheiferinn.co.uk

Lower Greenhill Caravan Park
Tel: 01282 813067
www.ukcamp.com

Monks House B&B
Tel: 01282 814423
www.barnoldswickguesthouse.co.uk

Gisburn
Foxhill Barn B&B
Tel: 01200 415906
www.foxhillbarn.co.uk

The White Bull
Tel: 01200 445155
www.whitebullgisburn.co.uk

THE YORKSHIRE DALES PART 1
LONG PRESTON TO
HORTON-IN-RIBBLESDALE

Long Preston
Maypole Inn
Tel: 01729 840219
www.maypole.co.uk

The Boars Head Hotel
Tel: 01729 840217
www.boarsheadlongpreston.co.uk

The Post Office and Store B&B
Tel: 01729 840335
http://home.btconnect.com/
longprestonpostoffice

Settle
Burn Lodge B&B
Tel: 01729 823118
www.yorkshirenet.co.uk/stayat/burnlodge

Hornby Laithe Bunkhouse Barn
Tel: 01729 8222240
www.yorkshirenet.co.uk/ydales/
bunkbarns/hornbylaithe

Knight Stainforth Hall Camping and
Caravan Park
Tel: 01729 822200
www.knightstainforth.co.uk

The Lion
Tel: 01729 822203
www.thelionsettle.co.uk

Austwick and Clapham
Dalesbridge – Camping, Bunkhouses, B&B
Tel: 01524 251021
www.dalesbridge.co.uk

The Game Cock Inn, Austwick
Tel: 01524 251226
www.gamecockinn.co.uk

Brookhouse Guest House, Clapham
Tel: 01524 251580
www.brookhouse-clapham.co.uk

The New Inn, Clapham
Tel: 01524 251203
www.newinn-clapham.co.uk

THE YORKSHIRE DALES PART 2
HORTON-IN-RIBBLESDALE TO
GARSDALE HEAD

Horton-in-Ribblesdale
Crown Hotel
Tel: 01729 860209
www.crown-hotel.co.uk

The Golden Lion Hotel and Bunkhouse
Tel: 01729 860206
www.goldenlionhotel.co.uk

Holme Farm Campsite
Tel: 01729 860281
www.ukcampsite.co.uk

The Willows B&B
Tel: 01729 860200
www.thewillowshorton.co.uk

THE YORKSHIRE DALES PART 3
GARSDALE HEAD TO
RAVENSTONEDALE

Garsdale Head
Moorcock Inn
Tel: 01969 667488
www.moorcockinn.com

The Garsdale Luxury B&B
Tel: 01969 667096
www.thegarsdale.com

Yore House Farm Caravan and Camping
Tel: 01969 667358

Ravenstonedale
The Fat Lamb
Tel: 01539 623242
www.fatlamb.co.uk

The King's Head
Tel: 01539 623050
www.kings-head.com

The Black Swan Hotel
Tel: 01539 623204
www.blackswanhotel.com

Low Greenside Campsite
Tel: 01539 623217
rosie@lowgreenside.f9.co.uk

Bowber Head Camping
Tel: 01539 623254
http://hiddenhowgills.co.uk/accom/
camping.html

*The River Clough, Garsdale
(Section 3 Route 9; photo: EA Bowness)*

Gayle Beck (Section 3 Route 7)

Appendix E
Bike shops

Hebden Bridge
Blazing Saddles
Tel: 01422 844435
Email: info@blazingsaddles.co.uk
www.blazingsaddles.co.uk

Burnley
On Yer Bike Cycles
Tel: 01282 438855
Email: info@onyerbikeonline.com

Colne
Fox's Cycles
Tel: 01282 863017
www.foxscycles.co.uk

Wicked Cycles
Tel: 01282 863089
Email: sales@wickedcycles.co.uk
www.wickedcycles.co.uk

Barnoldswick
Bruffy's Bikes
Tel: 01282 813308
Mob: 07962055475
Email: Bruffybike@hotmail.com

Skipton
The Bicycle Shop
Tel: 01756 794386
Email: sales@bicycleshop.co.uk
www.bicycleshop.co.uk

Gisburn
Gisburn Forest Bikes
Tel: 01729 840668
Email: bikemad@gisburnforestbikes.co.uk
www.gisburnforestbikes.co.uk

Settle
3 Peaks Cycles
Tel: 01729 824232
Email: sales@3peakscycles.com
www.3peakscycles.com

Westhouse, near Ingleton
Escape Bike Shop
Tel: 015242 41226
Email: sales@escapebikeshop.com
www.escapebikeshop.com

Kirkby Stephen
Kirkby Stephen Cycle Centre
Tel: 017683 71658
Email: exploreoutdoor@aol.com

The Yorkshire Dales
The Dales Bike Doctor
Tel: 07540 403455
www.dalesbikedoctor.co.uk

A mobile bike repair service who will travel to your location and repair your bike wherever you happen to be. He will give a quotation over the telephone before travelling out to solve your mechanical problems. Based near Ingleton, The Dales Bike Doctor will cover all areas accessed by the Pennine Bridleway from Barnoldswick in the south to Ravenstonedale in the north.

Notes

Notes

Listing of Cicerone Guides

For full information on all our
guides, and to order books and
eBooks, visit our website:
www.cicerone.co.uk.

Walking – Trekking – Mountaineering – Climbing – Cycling

Over 40 years, Cicerone have built up an outstanding collection of 300 guides, inspiring all sorts of amazing adventures.

 Every guide comes from extensive exploration and research by our expert authors, all with a passion for their subjects. They are frequently praised, endorsed and used by clubs, instructors and outdoor organisations.

All our titles can now be bought as **e-books** and many as iPad and Kindle files and we will continue to make all our guides available for these and many other devices.

Our website shows any **new information** we've received since a book was published. Please do let us know if you find anything has changed, so that we can pass on the latest details. On our **website** you'll also find some great ideas and lots of information, including sample chapters, contents lists, reviews, articles and a photo gallery.

It's easy to keep in touch with what's going on at Cicerone, by getting our monthly **free e-newsletter**, which is full of offers, competitions, up-to-date information and topical articles. You can subscribe on our home page and also follow us on **Facebook** and **Twitter**, as well as our **blog**.

Cicerone – the very best guides for exploring the world.

CICERONE

2 Police Square Milnthorpe Cumbria LA7 7PY
Tel: 015395 62069 info@cicerone.co.uk
www.cicerone.co.uk